D0729714

YAPPY Days

Behind the Scenes with Newsers, Schmoozers, Boozers and Losers

Bernadette Duncan

authorHOUSE®

*AuthorHouse™
1663 Liberty Drive
Bloomington, IN 47403
www.authorhouse.com
Phone: 1 (800) 839-8640*

*Talkers Books
785 Williams Street, #429
Longmeadow, Massachusetts 01106
www.Talkers.com
Phone: 413-565-5413*

Published by AuthorHouse 09/27/2016

*ISBN: 978-1-5246-0053-2 (sc)
ISBN: 978-1-5246-0052-5 (hc)
ISBN: 978-1-5246-0054-9 (e)*

Library of Congress Control Number: 2016906568

Printed in the USA

This book is printed on acid-free paper.

To my husband Michael, whose love, companionship and conversation I value more than anything. Everything good in my life is because of you.

Author's Note

Everything you're about to read has happened to me – but some events have been compressed so to strengthen the narrative flow. All dialogue was recreated to the best of my ability, in some cases from notes. While many of the well-known people are mentioned here by name, the events we shared are clearly my perspective only.

Contents

Author's Note vii

Preface xi

Chapter One
So, What Exactly is a Talk Show Producer? 1
Chapter Two
You Talkin' to Me? 8
Chapter Three
Brushes with Rushes 16
Chapter Four
They Eat Producers, Don't They? 29
Chapter Five
Sally Go 'Round the Roses 36
Chapter Six
King and I 56
Chapter Seven
The Art of the Schmooze 73
Chapter Eight
Gil Who? 79
Chapter Nine
Stories and Guests that
Just Wouldn't Go Away 88
Chapter Ten
Bowties and Poetry 93
Chapter Eleven
Bushy Eyebrows (and Then Some) 100
Chapter Twelve
Took a Leap 117
Chapter Thirteen
Another Day, Another Terror 127

Chapter Fourteen
Where's the Satellite? 141
Chapter Fifteen
Talk Show, Freak Show 144
Chapter Sixteen
Expanding Horizons 168
Chapter Seventeen
The Politics of Political Guests 176
Chapter Eighteen
It's Only a Job Interview 199
Chapter Nineteen
Feuds, Stress and Lessons Learned 208

Epilogue 223

Index 231

Acknowledgments 243

Preface

During my 26 years in broadcasting, I've had the opportunity to meet and work with conservative, liberal, moderate, and apolitical yappers who have collectively authored hundreds of books. My living room bookshelves buckle with their weight. Titles by Rush Limbaugh, Sean Hannity, Mark Levin, Alan Colmes, Thom Hartmann, Lou Dobbs, Mike Gallagher and dozens of others are all politically charged with the subtext "How to fix the economy," "Come on America, this is the answer," or "Here's what's RIGHT about US and WRONG about THEM."

Other hosts such as Larry King, Sally Jessy Raphael, and Charles Osgood weave charming childhood stories into their memoirs that deliver insights about what inspired their larger-than-life selves.

While informative and packed with dogma, most of these books often left me feeling short-changed. In most cases, these mouthy authors skipped the *human interest* aspects of what occurred behind the scenes. What happened during the commercial breaks, or when the wrong spot fired? What about when a guest walked out mid-interview? All kinds of things happen during the course of a radio show. I once returned to the studio from the top-of-the-hour newsbreak (a.k.a. "the bathroom break") and discovered I was locked out. The handles on both sides of the door had literally fallen off - and get this - the only one left in the control room was the intern. Talk about momentary panic! These kinds of incidents tend to reveal true character. This book is about the character of *characters*.

And, boy oh boy, did I work with characters. The pages ahead attempt to freeze-frame unexpected events such as my doorknob catastrophe, as well as encounters with celebrities and over-the-top nut-jobs I've worked with during my 1983 - 2009 talk show history. It also explores complex office politics that exist in this quirky arena of show business and communications. It captures a glimpse into the hardly-ever chronicled subject of what it takes to be a radio *producer* - the most under-rated, under-paid and under-appreciated job in audio media. It's about converting raw data and news stories into talking points for the host. It's about finding the right words to convey complicated truths to audiences with ever-decreasing attention spans. It's about being a gatekeeper, filtering what does and does not get on-air, as well as greeting the guests, greasing the skids and putting out the fires... and not always successfully.

I've corralled experiences from 26 years of being a news/talk show producer at ABC, CBS, NBC, Fox, and United Stations Radio Networks in addition to local New York City radio landmarks WOR and WMCA. I've culled stories from thousands of interviews, colorful behind-the-scenes moments and hope to present a better understanding of this process called "the talk show."

When the program's host could seamlessly navigate his or her way through the course of a show with thorough background materials, commercial copy, dynamic guests and a focused approach, I knew I had succeeded in keeping my job… at least for another day.

So here we go. It's time for the person "behind the glass" to talk. After all, the best part of spoken-word radio - both on and off the air - is *storytelling.* It's time somebody wrote a book from the producer's point of view, and maybe even spill a little.

Like talk radio itself, the pages that follow springboard from chatty to newsy and sometimes frenetic in the style of a yammering guide on a tour bus through the streets of the Big Apple. As they say in my world, "Sit back, relax and enjoy the show." Just maybe, to quote Brooke Gladstone of NPR's "On the Media," you'll get a fuller understanding of how the "talk radio sausage is assembled."

Chapter One

SO, WHAT EXACTLY IS A TALK SHOW PRODUCER?

There's nothing like an eyeball-to-eyeball confrontation with Geraldo Rivera to jumpstart a morning.

That's exactly what I discovered on launch day of "The Lou Dobbs Radio Show" in June 2008. Geraldo stormed into the green room, flanked by a camera crew. As the executive producer and "gatekeeper" on Dobbs' show, I had to convince Geraldo to halt, heel, and roll over. At the heart of the drama: I would not allow Geraldo's camera crew into the studio, *our* studio, to video his interview with Dobbs. He and my host had colossal differences of opinion over immigration issues - views they each had been dishing out independently on numerous other news and talk shows during preceding weeks, always mentioning the other's name in a disparaging manner. Now, on my first day of what was supposed to be a crown-jewel job with the CNN anchor, I was bulldogging Geraldo and Geraldo was trying to growl me into submission.

"You cannot bring in those cameras," I said in my best stone-cold manner.

"Oh yes I can," he snapped.

"Oh no you can't..."

"Oh yes I can..."

Meanwhile, the countdown clock was blinking. Four minutes became three, became two... until finally we made a truce.

I pleaded, "It's my first day on this job... my very first, please."

I must have looked as harried as I felt because Geraldo gave in - though only after we each signed a Dunkin' Donuts paper napkin on which he drew up an agreement stating that neither party would film this segment for future purposes. Besides being an award-winning newsman (170-plus honors over his 40 years) and nationally-famous talk show host, Geraldo is also an attorney.

It wouldn't be long before I'd resign from this new gig.

Variety and adrenaline

Over my 26 years as a TV and radio talk show producer working with celebrity hosts such as Larry King, Sally Jessy Raphael, Tom Snyder, and Charles Osgood, I've had plenty of opportunity to fuel my adrenaline. You might say it was my drug of choice since I switched careers three times (a stint into the film business for $10-an-hour and a couple of detours into television) only to come crawling back to producing radio. Like a true addict.

Plus, these were *my people*.

In this field, I've hunted down the latest gossip-page celebrities, the hottest political experts and news analysts, as well as the actual players in the sordid tales that hijacked the headlines and my life:

- Tiger's Twisted Double Life!

- John Edwards' Love Child Scandal!

- O.J. Simpson's Super Bowl Prison Party

...I could go on.

Sex tapes, celebrity cheaters, wife beaters, and White House meltdowns - these were just some of the gems that kept this wheel turning (and me employed). Some days I'd wonder what was wackier - the headlines that I covered or the hosts discussing them.

Welcome to my world and the issues that fueled my daily editorial meetings. "Talk Show Producer" is what I wrote on my IRS statement for nearly three decades. In reality, it was a lot more. As producer, I've:

-Calmed a shrill Joan Rivers at 6:55 am while she raged at me because of a very dense lineup of interviews scheduled to promote her new E! show, "Fashion Police."

-Begged the local cleaners to deliver comic Lewis Black's freshly pressed pants to the studio so he'd finish the interview and still make his plane on time.

-Raced after former US Attorney General John Ashcroft when he bolted from his chair during a two-hour, LIVE interview, leaving me with 42 minutes to fill.

-Coddled a suicidal caller from Brooklyn during a commercial break until I could connect him to the host, late-night talker Neil Myers, then committed the ultimate no-no of bumping commercials to the bottom of the hour, running 14 back-to-back (and I prayed that I'd still have a job the next day).

- Delivered numerous coffees (always black, one Sweet'N Low) to Larry King while he was in studio or out on yet another book tour in midtown Manhattan.

- Tracked down devil-worshippers in the back hills of Louisiana through a series of online searches until I got them on a flight to New York City.

- Wrangled with the receptionist at CBS to allow Joy Behar to bring her two dogs up to the studio - promising on the life of my first-born (if I ever had one) that I'd pick up any and all doodies.

- Packaged and returned a half-dozen cell phones to celebrities who accidentally left them behind in the studio - including one to a very drunk, well-known movie director who proceeded to falsely accuse me of hacking his contacts so I could steal celebrity phone numbers.

- Stalked presidential candidate John McCain at the February 2000 New Hampshire primary but only landed an interview with his teenage son.

Producers, I'm convinced, are a self-selecting group of individuals who are addicted to the "cram" (that is, the rush-rush-rush of deadlines) as much as the "glam" (the parade of celebs joining us on a daily basis).

Take the evening I helped comedian George Carlin adjust his headset and volume control. When all was set and in place, he looked me straight in the eye and asked, "I won't get a lethal disease from this, will I?" For the rest of the night, I kept pinching myself, wondering, *did George Carlin just joke around with me? Me? A girl from Queens?*

Something I learned about being a producer is that you don't need a specific skill as much as you need a wide net of temporary facts, a modicum of intelligence, and boundless energy.

You read multiple newspapers and magazines while placing phone calls to potential guests, confirming and re-confirming the day's line-up, fending off calls from publicists hyping inappropriate guests for the show. You listen anyway because the next time she calls, she may be offering the hottest reality show TV star and you must grease "the machine." Other times, you're patiently schmoozing a congressman's press person, sometimes the congressman him- or herself, all the while eyeballing the clock because you can never be late for a live show, pre-interview, or the next best guest you discover before someone else does. You're a jack-in-the-box ready to spring on the unexpected.

When you leave the office 10 or so hours later, you may be headed to a movie screening featuring a guest scheduled in studio the next morning; a best-selling author's reading at the local Barnes & Noble; or straight to your couch to rifle through the remaining news magazines or dailies that you barely scanned earlier at your desk. When you finally drop off to sleep at some witching hour, an LA-based publicist might call to say that your guest scheduled for that morning had to cancel. What happens next depends on your industrious, brainstorming capacity and ability to find a backup guest. Welcome to the "glam life."

What drives a radio talk show producer at heart? In most cases, it's far less the paycheck and much more the heart. Very few jobs pay like those with big talkers such as Rush Limbaugh, Sean Hannity or Glenn Beck in which a producer can snare a comfortable middle-class salary. There are many different pay scales and business models depending upon market ranking or show size. Some producers' salaries are based upon what's termed "revenue sharing" in which their incomes are in ratio to how much money their shows generate. Whatever the model, however, most shows pay less than the handful of big ones at the top. Way less… from a tough living all the way down to minimum wage.

So really, what was the appeal?

The reasons I first entered this field are not necessarily the reasons I stayed. Initially, I was swept up by the glam. Remember, I was only 20 years old. The reason I stuck around? Plain and simple: It was the "action." I valued the ongoing opportunity to work with hosts in delivering fresh ideas and hard truths about the complicated world in which we live. From that came tremendous personal growth. I was constantly challenged to tap into and improve upon a range of my own skills: newshound, writer, organizer, researcher, psychologist, air traffic controller, circus juggler - and sometimes even waitress.

For me, the driving force of a talk show was the host. He or she was a force field, charmed with supernatural powers and smarts - or at least that's what I thought when I started in the business as an intern at WMCA in New York City.

Eventually, I came to see them with all their human faults and witness this common belief so many of them shared - *it's more important to appear right than to tell the truth.* For me to dwell exclusively on that, though, would be somewhat hypocritical given that so much more of our media, politics and culture subscribe to that premise.

What I did learn along the way was that when conversations went haywire and melted down (which they often did), the true talent could step up, slap it, knead it, punch it up, then roll it out, while also having fun. After all, this was "entertainment" - and the good ones never forgot that.

Since I never found my way to sit behind the mic, I pulled up a chair on the team that supported the ones who did. I dealt with breaking news, misfired commercials or theme music mid-show, and in my world, learned to "change tires" in the middle of a breakdown... whatever it took to keep the conversation going.

Believe me, I got plenty of opportunity.

This is the story of what it's like to be on the frontline in the hot seat of a job known as talk show producer, dealing with dramas, egos, guests and time-crunching with the likes of Larry King, Lou Dobbs, Sally Jessy Raphael, Tom Snyder, Charles Osgood, and others. In reality, it was like the guy who used to spin the plates atop the poles on the old "Ed Sullivan Show."

Looking back, I can say, if you'll pardon the expression, "mission accomplished." Well, at least on most days.

Chapter Two

YOU TALKIN' TO ME?

To survive in broadcasting's number one market, a local New York show must capture the heart and soul of the city itself, but most importantly, the voice of its people... New *Yawkers*. For most of its 17 years, the *Daily News* "Bulldog Edition" on WOR was one of the highest-rated shows in its time slot and featured an assortment of Brooklyn-Queens-Bronx-Staten Island-Manhattan accents. The reporters were the real deal. You can't fake real on radio. Especially not to born-and-bred Big Apple listeners.

The secret formula for this show lasting all those years? These reporters had "street cred." They delivered their stories "in a New York minute" and made you laugh along the way. The "Bulldog Edition," a name referring to the earliest edition of a print newspaper, was the evening drive radio show which brought the listener into a city newsroom 60 minutes before deadline and a solid 11 hours before it thumped on the front stoop at home. In the days before the internet, a steady flow of reporters highlighted the hot news on-air from the next day's paper.

A real life Lou Grant

What made the show snap was the bespectacled, cigar-chomping Dick Oliver, a veteran at the *News* for over 20 years - his last three as assistant managing editor. He was the old-style city editor, a workaholic "man's man" with the backbone of a tough loner. A Lou Grant. Oliver was baptized by the dramas of the 1960s - covering Jack

Kennedy's rise to senator to president and then icon... later to Vietnam, and then the recession of the 1970s and more. His "war stories" spoke to a reporter's life well-lived. He was as much beloved for his news judgment and smarts (both his undergraduate and graduate degree were from Columbia University) as he was for his pranks and colorful nature.

One story he told from his cub reporter days back in the late-1960s inspired a New York tradition, which is still around today. On the eve of the world famous St. Patrick's Day Parade, he and two buddies secretly rolled green paint over the center yellow line that ran down Fifth Avenue. Attendants the next day were so tickled by this that the "rolling of the green" is still part of the parade prep.

When I first met "Oli," the nickname most everyone called him, the producer leaving the job whispered out of range, "Don't let him scare you. Just 'cruise' with whichever Oliver shows up on any given day - whether the surly one, the introverted professor, or the prankster."

It seemed everyone else took this approach. Oliver juggled a troupe of wise-asses, er, reporters, on-air whose bylines included Pulitzer-nominated Alex Michelini (whose loud-mouthed manner belied his five-foot stature); Larry Sutton who was on a first-name basis with every politician and celebrity in town (which paved his future career path to *People* magazine); Jerry Capese, whose "Gangland" column covered the latest rub-outs by the local mob families (whose sources included underworld family members, victims, prosecutors, and FBI agents); feature writer Hank Gallo (who went on to produce "The Daily Show"); and a married couple whose gossip column was titled "Rush & Molloy" (that's George and Joanna). Also along for the broadcast was John Marzulli, who covered local crime from One Police Plaza, otherwise known as "The Shack" due to its scrubby decor. He became so enraptured with police culture that he swapped his press credentials for a police badge, only to leave the force after eight years and return to the newspaper and his old job with greater insight. On Fridays, sports cartoonist Bill Gallo chatted with us from his art studio/office, where he churned out over 15,000 pieces in pen and ink during a 50-year career.

For a rookie 28-year-old newsie like me back in 1988, this job was primo, or so I thought. After all, this was New York, the number one media market with its ethnic diversity and constant stream of social and political hot buttons - from pooper-scooper laws to Donald Trump's hairdo and marriages, to tales from Studio 54 or Sam the Cabbie.

To pull together a two-hour show, I "worked the newsroom," designing my rundown from the projected headline stories listed on the ever-changing computerized "white board." Every reporter logged into it and that board was my brain center - it was magical. Also at my fingertips were the ever-breaking stories from various bureaus around the country, including Washington, DC and Los Angeles, as well as wire services such as AP News and Reuters. On any given day, I'd be racing through the newsroom, assigning on-air times to various reporters who were always vying for an invite onto the show. Each report added $25 to their paycheck - some earned an extra $500 a month.

"Today's reporters - they don't get jack at Starbucks"

Of course, there were the "satellite offices" as well - various "watering holes" where reporters unwound at the end of their hairy long days, but still conducted business on a more informal level. Let's just say I was likely the only

New York-based producer who kept a phone list of every drinking establishment in Manhattan tacked to the wall above her desk. By day's end, I'd locate certain big-name columnists and reporters by calling directly to the bar. My first day on the job, just after I was given a photo-I.D. to enter the building, I had to swear on my life to various reporters that I would never disclose the details on that list. Not to anyone. Especially wives.

"If you do," one crusty reporter threatened in front of three others, "you'll find yourself nailed to the wall just like that list of numbers." Everyone laughed when he said it, so I did too. However, I was sure he wasn't kidding.

As the new kid at the paper - and often the only female in the studio - I was fishing in uncharted waters, the stuff I somehow missed in journalism class. There were rules to learn. "Bars were for 'research,'" that same red-eyed reporter said while pouring Hennessy into his coffee at lunch hour.

The fact is these "outposts" allowed reporters to hobnob with firemen, cops, up-and-coming politicians, and all kinds of celebrities. As one veteran later pointed out, "You never know who'll walk through the door and lead you to a front page story. Today's reporters - they don't get jack at Starbucks."

Down in the basement

Speaking of outposts - the actual physical location for the studio and show was seven floors below ground from the City Room in a subterranean location in the historic landmarked art deco building on 42nd Street (said to be the model for the *Daily Planet* of "Superman" movie fame). Every day, I'd snake my way through the back of the building, descending by way of the delivery elevator, which opened up to a dark musty hallway with exposed piping and hanging bulbs. Perhaps purposefully - the actual door to the studio was unmarked.

Inside the crammed, windowless 9 x 12 space was a scrappy orange couch (plucked from a trash bin one avenue over), a yellowish (or was it brown?) thread-bare loveseat, three bar stools, and two 1950s-type blue vinyl chairs with exposed stuffing, all facing a gnarly old-fashioned wooden desk manned nightly by our anchorman and news director, the aforementioned Dick Oliver. My new boss.

Wall-hangings - mostly stolen from local bars - covered the peeling paint beneath. My official studio clock was in the shape of a large plastic Heineken beer bottle. Also surrounding us were a Coors Light tin sign, a Pilsner banner, a number of Rolling Rock hats and coasters, a row of baseball caps with various team emblems, political posters from elections over the years, favorite cartoons from the paper, T-shirts featuring Superman or Batman and Robin, and an array of unclaimed keys. If something were lost, found or stolen - it made its way to that wall.

Whenever an important work-related notice was faxed to my attention - such as commercial copy to be read live on-air that evening - Oliver hammered it to the wall (with his shoe) just behind his desk. I knew just where to look.

With cigars and cigarettes dangling from their mouths, a core cast of five or six reporters perched themselves in their usual spots, transforming the space into a smoky clubhouse. There was logic to the system. I just had to figure it out. The key to being a good producer? Know that the logic starts with the host.

Understanding Oli

To understand Oliver, all I had to do was flip on the TV before sunrise. His "morning job" was news correspondent for WNYW-TV's "Good Day New York." Long before most morning alarms sounded, he was already patrolling his way through one of New York's five boroughs, chasing a breaking story - a helicopter crash, the aftermath of a fire, the start of a school riot, or the latest bloody find in Central Park. Little wonder why he'd often be sprawled out on the studio couch napping when I arrived with rundown in hand ready to get the show on-air. Oliver lived two-and-a-half lives rolled into one.

Learning the nuances of any new job can be staggering - but this one was loaded with idiosyncrasies. I tip-toed through my first few days on the job, learning the computer system and studio technology, writing the daily headlines and rundown, juggling the traffic, stock market and weather reporters - all while coordinating city room reporters with those at the satellite offices. And then of course, there was Oliver.

Was this job really worth $9-an-hour (about twice the minimum wage in 1988)? Would I, could I, ever "get it" all? Why was I becoming more and more crabby?

Maybe, I concluded four days into the job, I wasn't cut out for this work. Every evening, before the "on-air" light went on and while cigar fumes filled the room, Oliver morphed into Lou Grant while reviewing my news copy, slashing words with a grizzly "hrumph!" followed up with an exasperated "Why can't producers spell?" If I didn't implode from all the on-the-job smoke, I was sure I'd eventually keel over from the anxiety.

What gave me the security to consider quitting was my "second" job moonlighting at CBS - which in broadcasting is common, given the unpredictability of the business. By week two, as the vibe worsened, I was ready. My plan was to bail out that Friday.

Sure enough, on that day, Oliver wanted his copy and he wanted it now. "Come on already!" he demanded in front of everyone. As the pressure mounted inside me, I handed him his copy and an unexpected volley of *lip*. In language he'd understand.

"Fuck you, Oliver!"

Silence.

A roomful of chatty reporters was instantaneously dumbfounded. Men and women who had witnessed murder scenes and gruesome car crashes were paralyzed. Not only did I stun everyone else, I also stunned myself. I *never* swore! My previous job was writing copy and features at squeaky-clean *Seventeen* magazine. Nobody, I mean *nobody,* ever spoke to Oliver that way. Until now.

Oliver, facing me with a slow-growing smile and a cigar clenched in his teeth, applauded. "Welcome to the *Daily News,*" he said. "We were wondering if you had it in you."

That moment changed me forever. I found my voice and the courage to use it. Just as important, I realized that yes, news was serious business, but you can also have fun delivering it - especially behind-the-scenes. Oliver knew how to have fun - though sometimes at the expense of the new kid on staff.

Over the next eight years, Oli and his rollicking gang of reporters volleyed through the most remarkable headline news stories that made New York the number one broadcasting town in the nation. And yes, on occasion, reporters showed up with fumes of Heineken on their breath.

When a reporter overdid it, I'd get THE CALL on the studio "hotline" from the program director (PD) of the station, my boss, Ed Walsh. Normally calm, he'd be shouting, "One beer, he sounds fine. But after that, sloppy. Do you understand?"

Which yes, I understood. But that didn't mean I knew what to do about it or could - even if I did.

Getting wise

Let's just say, I learned great negotiating skills. (Note: Child-rearing psychology works effectively in moments like this with reporters and talk show hosts.) During the next commercial break, I'd repeat the directive as stated by the PD and then add, "Of course, do what you want, after all it's only your *job*." Everyone got the message.

And while they sobered up, I grew up. What happened inside me was that I tapped into one of the toughest responsibilities of being a talk show producer - protecting your talent and their reputations. For their own good. Even when they didn't realize it.

In looking back over those eight years, here's the wisdom I carried the rest of my career: Sometimes the most challenging job a producer can have is one that's most worth the effort. Little did I know at the time, this wasn't so much a job but boot camp for a lifetime of challenging personalities and their talk shows. Whether it was Tom, Lou, Larry, or Sally, I grew to quickly identify and understand the ego, then help mold the talker into the best that he or she could be.

Easily said.

Chapter Three

BRUSHES WITH RUSHES

If it weren't for Rush Limbaugh, the modern era of talk radio that has been described as a phenomenon that "saved the AM band" (or at least forestalled its eventual demise by at least three decades) might not have ever gotten off the ground.

Every generation of entertainers in all genres of media, let alone talk radio, *needs* a Rush Limbaugh... though few on the liberal side of the talk radio divide may want to admit that.

However, when Rush is bad, he's *bad* - unless you subscribe to the philosophy that all publicity, however controversial or even scandalous, is good.

The four wives!

The Viagra incident!

Countless on-air remarks that outrage the sensibilities of most on the left, many in the middle, and even some on the right!

Sandra Fluke!

When Rush is good - that is, when he rants about his philosophies and articulates a point of view that resonates with millions of Americans - he provides listeners with a reason to applaud, hate, rally, laugh, question, disagree... and, of course, think.

Love him or hate him, he has generated advertising dollars and non-stop press year after year in a potentially dying medium (advertiser boycotts over the Sandra Fluke "slut" incident notwithstanding) and has brought significant attention to the entire platform of talk radio as wielding political and social influence. For any host, television or radio, left or right, that's a formidable accomplishment.

When the *New York Daily News* sent me out to interview Rush Limbaugh in December 1991, no one could have predicted how iconic he would become in this business.

Rush Limbaugh 1.0

Once upon a time, Rush was a boy-faced, 320 pound, 40-year-old with choirboy politeness, standing 5'11", his hair perfectly parted to one side. In three years broadcasting to the nation from New York City, he stirred up plenty of attention. Is it possible that a bully (in the opinion of many) conservative talker in a liberal town could be - *successful?*

"Even people who disagree with him listen," my editor, Fran Wood, said as she assigned me to investigate the man behind the growing affiliate numbers. (He started in August 1988 with 56 affiliated stations that ballooned at a phenomenal pace.) By 1990, *TALKERS* magazine was tracking his affiliates in the hundreds.

"I'm sending a photographer with you, but maybe you really need a bodyguard," she joked before I left.

I quickly learned that I shouldn't judge a host by his "bully conservative" shtick. About the only thing in my face about Rush that morning was his splashy Crayola-colored necktie. (Years later, Rush and wife number three would start the "No Boundaries" line of ties and rake in a reported five million bucks before both the marriage and the business dissolved.) I noted - Rush wore a tie to a radio station. (A tie? On radio?) It said a lot.

In person, he was neither flashy nor shy. As we sat in the small windowless office with bland industrial furniture, his intermittent eye contact suggested thoughtfulness. He wasn't looking to schmooze me or impress me with words or awards. He was simply telling me his back-story.

Raised in Cape Girardeau, Missouri, he started in radio at 16. Years later, he landed in Sacramento where he replaced Morton Downey Jr. at local station KFBK. The self-described "workaholic" confessed, "I never went out socially unless it was business-related." He was discovered by Ed McLaughlin, the former president of ABC Radio who launched a well-connected boutique syndication firm (EFM Media Management) in 1988 with Limbaugh's show the first out of the gate. This story is quite well-known having been told in radio circles countless times.

But really, when I had my first brush with Rush, he was just getting hatched. This was the pre-headline-rousing Rush Limbaugh - the *funny* Rush.

I followed him into the studio as bluesy intro music filled the air and kicked off the show. Seated with eyes closed, he crooned along with "My City Was Gone" by the Pretenders. He later explained that this became his choice for the opening theme music because of the irony of a conservative like him using an anti-conservative song. He fell back into his chair with the lyrics "*...I went back to Ohio but my city was gone...*" and his doughy left hand drummed the table strewn with newspaper clippings.

When the "on-air" light popped on, the "pronunciator" (his word) reminded listeners across the country that his "talent was on loan from God." During the first commercial break, we talked numbers. Rush said that just three years on the network, he had already accumulated 440 affiliates - and according to *TALKERS*, his audience outnumbered the combined total of the second and third most popular hosts, Bruce Williams and Larry King. The *combined* total.

Okay. This guy was a phenom… and his success would spawn a dozen, if not more, reasonably successful copycats.

But this guy was also complex. Rush made choices as a host that were counter-intuitive to most others. An example I witnessed as I sat in studio: callers who disagreed with him were shuffled to the front of the line to go on the air immediately. As Rush often joked (and sometimes even on air), "I'm on a mission to help the poor and suffering in America," whose liberal views were "taking them down." Another example of how he stood out in those early days from other so-called combative conservative hosts was that he would *politely* disagree with liberal callers. Or at least until they hung up.

To further promote his opinions, Rush featured song parodies and skits with an army of voice actors doing imitations of Bill Clinton, George Bush, and Dick Cheney, just to name a few (many performed by comic Paul Shankin). Rush also introduced the terms "Femi-Nazis!" (translation: militant NOW members), "environmental wackos!" (translation: ecology activists), and "commie-pinko libs" (anyone left of him). He and his team had a backlog of skits that lampooned and poked fun at one or all of them. Well, fun for those who were not the butts of his jokes.

But was Rush kidding? I mean, *really* kidding? Yes. No. Maybe.

Exactly. And that was clever shtick. Both hate-mongers and fans of satire alike could listen to Rush rant, yet arrive at different interpretations. And that's not all.

If I learned anything that day, it was that Rush was a walking, talking paradox – and it showed itself in the details he shared.

He was friends with both straight-laced Republican Ronald Reagan speechwriter Peggy Noonan *and* headline catching Mayflower Madame Sidney Biddles Barrow. He quit college after only a year - yet a listener often needed a college education to follow the show's content. By age 40, he had been married and divorced twice, explaining, "I guess I'm not meant to be married." (Twenty-plus years later - by the time he was 61 - he would be married twice more.)

The only question I asked that caused Rush to be momentarily speechless was, "If you were magically reincarnated as a woman, whom would you hope that to be?" Finally piping up, he said, "Former Ambassador to the U.N., (and first female to land the job) Jeanne Kirkpatrick," who also held a staunch anti-communist stand.

But the real clincher of the day came just before I left the station when I stopped in to chat with WABC's liberal talker, the late Lynn Samuels. As one of Rush's colleagues at the station, she offered this insight, "I think everything he says is off-the-wall. But I love Rush. He's just very sweet. Though he's not going to like that I'm saying this, I think he's very insecure."

Sweet? Did Lynn call Rush *sweet*? "Sweet" was not a word that came to my mind.

Before long, another word would be associated with Rush - "giant."

Rush 1.0 was a rising giant in talk - though no one could have predicted how gigantic he'd become.

Rush Limbaugh 2.0

In addition to his ever-increasing salary during those early days (both $300,000 and $500,000 have been quoted over the years), Rush took his show on the road in what he called "Rush to Excellence" tours, making as much as $25,000 a shot. These were live stage performances where listeners could watch him take on issues of the day. Before long, Rush's books, *The Way Things Ought To Be* (Pocket Books, 1992) and *I Told You So* (Altria, 1993), both zoomed right to the top of *The New York Times* best-seller list.

While he only authored two books, a flood of writers followed with works that featured his name in the title. In the *title!* At least 30 are still listed on Amazon, such as Al Franken's *Rush Limbaugh Is a Big Fat Idiot* (Delacourt, 1996) and Zev Chafets' *Rush Limbaugh: An Army of One* (Sentinel HC, 2010).

Rush was both a commodity and a brand. It was why Republican media mogul Roger Ailes (who would later develop the Fox News Channel) signed Rush to host "Rush Limbaugh the TV Show," a late-night half-hour program. While it only lasted four years (1992-1996), Rush blanketed his brand elsewhere, including a line of cigars, coffee mugs, bumper stickers and T-shirts. He even produced a monthly subscription newsletter (which still exists) at $29.95 a pop.

Before long, he was a household name - even at the White House. Just for the record, Rush's show was not designed to include guests - after all, he said, "This is not a show where we care to find out what America thinks. This is a show about what *I* think, what *I'm* interested in." Except if your name was George H. W. Bush, George W. Bush, or Dan Quayle. They are among the very few guests Rush has ever had on his show. In return, in 1992, Rush was invited for an overnight stay at the White House - and George 41 made a show of it for the press by carrying the talk show host's overnight bags up to the famous Lincoln Bedroom. (How many other radio hosts can say they stayed in the Lincoln Bedroom? Don't bother Googling it - the answer is zero.)

Ironically, when Bill Clinton made it to the White House and the "enemy camp" took over, Rush's ratings sky-rocketed - kicking off a wave of combativeness as a ratings-getting technique in talk media. As luck had it (for Rush, at least), President Clinton regularly engaged the media star in public debate, elevating the "mere" talk host to a national level that millions of dollars of advertisement could not buy. The President of the United States was battling Rush Limbaugh and that must have meant, well, Rush was *important*.

He took the prodding and ran with it. In fact, the more run-ins with the White House, the better. News outlets branded this special dynamic between President Clinton and Rush the "War of Words" and it continued between the two long after Clinton left office. It happened so regularly back in the day of Rush's TV show that the producers actually listed Bill Clinton as "Head Writer" on the program's credits.

Politicos on both sides of the aisle, listeners on radio, news junkies, and the greater public were paying more and more notice to this talker.

Rush Limbaugh 3.0

A funny thing happened to Rush on his way to higher ratings. Every few months or so, a blistering revelation about him would break in the news and burn for days.

"Limbaugh admits addiction to pain medication" - CNN.com - October 2003

"Did popping painkillers make Rush lose his hearing?" - Salon.com – October 2003

"Talk host Limbaugh to enter drug rehab" - *Palm Beach Post* - November 2003

"Limbaugh, third wife parting after 10 years" - *Palm Beach Post* - June 2004

"Rush Limbaugh arrested on drug charges" - CBS News - April 2006

"Rush Limbaugh's Dominican stag party" - The Smoking Gun - July 2006

"Rush cleared in Viagra probe" - The Smoking Gun - July 2006

"Limbaugh signs through 2016; $400 million deal shatters broadcast records" - Drudgereport.com - July 2008

"Sandra Fluke, Georgetown student called 'slut' by Rush Limbaugh"- *Washington Post* - March 2012

"Rush Limbaugh loses 45 advertisers" - Politico.com - March 2012

Despite one explosive headline after another, Rush's popularity (and notoriety) continued to rise. His listener numbers grew, as evidenced by the ballooning 620 affiliates, as did his market value and lifestyle. Rush was now living in a $34 million home in Palm Beach, Florida on a private beach with three guesthouses and a guard station as well as a 10-room condominium on Manhattan's Fifth Avenue with a fireplace and direct elevator entry. He sold the condo in 2010 for $11.75 million.

These same marks of success also forced him into a life of hiding, to travel the world with security guards and strategize his safety right down to the studio from where he did his daily broadcasts.

Some 12 or so years after my initial brush with Rush for the *New York Daily News*, I was in West Palm Beach for business and my friend James Golden, a producer at the Rush Limbaugh Show, invited me to drop by. Rush himself was not there on this occasion.

Upon arriving at the office building in early-January 2004, one thing became immediately clear - how easily Rush dodged the paparazzi who scoured Palm Beach after his return from detox in November 2003. The so-called "Southern Command," the name Rush gave to his Palm Beach studio, was hardly the "heavily fortified bunker" he occasionally described on-air. Simply put, Rush had been hiding in full view - for years.

The designated parking spots and the door to the offices and studio were still inscribed with the previous tenant's name. Absolutely nothing indicated that Limbaugh roamed the halls. Nor was there a security guard or receptionist to ask which way to go because, well, they didn't exist either. The only thing "Limbaugh-ish" about the location was a lone American flag that stood in the corner of the mahogany-laden foyer.

It was all so very presidential. Even the conference room, which doubled as a dining area, had the aura of a Commander-in-Chief with its rich reddish brown table that nearly ran the length of the room, the glass cabinetry along one wall, and subtle lighting overhead.

James - who was (and still is) absolutely devoted to his boss - shared with me his first and only words with Rush after the host's 30-day absence and detox following the big "drug scandal." The discussion, he said, took place with Rush in the studio and while he was in the control room on the other side of the glass. Through the talk-back, he asked Rush, "You okay?"

"Yep," he responded.

And that was that. That was the extent of their conversation on "the subject" - and probably the very reason this producer was originally hired and is still employed today. Smart producers develop a sixth sense about a host and a skill to know when nothing said is saying quite enough. Work as closely as producers do with a talent and a word like "yep" is loaded with meaning. You learn to read the body language, connect through eye contact and most important, your gut.

Fast forward

Fast forward a few years to my next brush with Rush. This time at the *TALKERS* 2011 "New Media Seminar." Gone was the boy-face, the kind of shy sweetness, the pastiness, and yes, even the weight. Since the first time I met Rush in 1991, he had shed nearly 100 pounds and was now about 210 pounds. It was as if a new man stepped out from a fleece-lined overcoat. His hair was slicked back like Superman's and wisps of gray framed his ears, perfectly matching his gray linebacker-fit sports jacket. His sterling white pressed shirt was opened two buttons down. Rush was polished.

As he crossed the stage, the silence of anticipation in the room broke into a growing roar and applause, whistles and screams. The audience, comprised mostly of program directors, station owners, talk show hosts and producers, rose from their chairs in Super Bowl-like madness. They appreciated (maybe loved) what Rush had done for the industry. In three words, *he saved it.*

Rush stood at the podium, in complete control, smiling as multiple cameras fired off. At one point he even did a mock "glam pose," mugging a few times. He was now the recipient of the Freedom of Speech Award.

According to my husband - *TALKERS* publisher Michael Harrison - "Rush is a phenomenon like the Beatles. Before Rush Limbaugh, talk radio was a 'boutique' format on the sidelines of music radio. He has been to talk what Elvis was to rock 'n' roll. He wasn't the only person to make it happen - just the most important. He contributed greatly to saving the AM dial."

Rush 3.0 was among his people. Sure, he had stumbled a few times through the marshland of celebrity where detractors hoped to take him down. Yet, here he stood. He took one step in front of the other to show up on that stage. He has and had lived life on his terms, however fragile it seemed at times. Even when he went deaf in 2001, which some experts associated with his prescription drug (OxyContin) addiction. Today with a cochlear implant, he says he can hear, though it was reported in *The New York*

Times that a transcriber sits in studio with him during the show to instantly relay the caller's words.

Most recent brush

Troubled. Discomfort. Dark. These were three words that came to mind as I stood among approximately 50 radio broadcasters during an invitation-only photo session with the mega-star. It was September 2013 and the Rush Limbaugh who was standing several feet away appeared full of pain, a troubled and agitated expression building up on his face as he approached the front of the room. This was no longer the boy-faced man from Cape Girardeau. Nor was this the slick, confident icon who received the Freedom of Speech Award just a couple of years earlier. This man was still traveling with bodyguards and looked weary for it.

As the roomful of friendly business associates and radio station affiliates faced his direction, he passed within inches of me and appeared as if he were "walking the plank." We were a kind of inner circle to *this* Rush Limbaugh. Though in my case, I was really more a friend to a friend of the inner sanctum. Rush sure looked heavy with worry. As did his producer, Kit Carson, standing within earshot, as he always had since the early-1980s. Unfortunately, shortly after this, Kit Carson passed away at the age of 58 due to a brain tumor. Rush knew by this point that his most trusted staffer was battling brain cancer.

When I was invited to have a photo with the "big guy," he mugged to the camera making funny faces while everyone watched. He was not so much warm and fuzzy, but rather self-aware. I got the feeling that deep, down inside, he actually did not want to be there. Rush Limbaugh seemed to be a broadcaster most comfortable within the safety of the studio, doing what he does best - talking into a mic.

No doubt, Rush has paid a price for his celebrity. The question that remains and one that *The New York Times* asked in a 2010 magazine article: "Is Rush Limbaugh just getting warmed up?"

Time will tell. Perhaps there's a Rush 4.0 coming up right after the next station break.

Chapter Four

THEY EAT PRODUCERS, DON'T THEY?

If you've ever been part of the supposed 2% of the listening audience who call into a radio talk show, you were greeted by someone just like me… or perhaps someone NOT like me. In this business, the title "producer" often means different things in different situations. In many, it includes the tedious job of screening callers. Programs hosted by Glenn Beck, Rush Limbaugh, or Jim Bohannon can raise the process of choosing the right on-air caller to a religious experience. And yes, when the calls offered "slim pickings" (like the night of the Super Bowl), I have prayed.

Spacey environment

Back in the 1980s, when I first stepped into the studio at the NBC Radio Networks, I thought I landed inside the Starship Enterprise. The place hummed with electronics - all the gizmos it takes to deliver a show up to the satellite and across the United States. There were three computer monitors, numerous CD decks, at least three cart machines to play commercials, two reel-to-reel recorders to repeat the show overnight, an equalizer that added a weighty bass to a host's voice if requested, and at least 400 flickering lights in reds and yellows. Eventually, I would understand at least some of their purpose.

(Many of the aforementioned components are now obsolete having been replaced by sleeker - but still imposing - digital equipment.)

The first night, I shadowed a woman named Nancy, the screener/producer on the "Sally Jessy Raphael Show." She sat me in the hot seat next to her, both of us facing "the monstrosity," that is, the state-of-the-art 1970s phone bank with 10 flickering lines.

"Your goal," she directed me, "is to race through as many lines as you can to find the best next caller. It's okay to lie and, if you must, be rude... just rifle through. We didn't hire you to be the bubbly counterperson you see on a McDonald's TV commercial."

It was our boss, the program director, Dave Bartlett, who added, "If I *never* ever get a complaint about you, then you're not doing your job. Your goal is to keep callers *off* the air, not necessarily to put them on."

The selection process

The idea was to troll for a "good call," whatever *that* meant. I stared at the phone bank as Nancy gave me the lowdown on how to identify the rejects - those who:

1. Spoke with a thick accent.
2. Giggled while talking to you. (This could signal a potential crank.)
3. Slurred. (Translation: one too many glasses of wine).
4. Recited poetry.
5. Debated abortion. (The reason: it was an issue that never got resolved.)
6. Pushed (or denounced) religious issues - like the existence of God. (Refer back to reason #5.)

7. Refused to turn off their radio, not realizing they would cause delayed audio or feedback. (Before clearing someone for air, we always asked one more time, "Is your radio off?")
8. Only used speakerphone (thus reducing the on-air quality of sound).
9. Wished to compliment the host and *only* compliment the host. (I know, I know - this sounds counter-intuitive. Of course, the host loved compliments, but this slowed down any momentum you wanted to build on a subject.)
10. Were "regulars" (which we tried to limit) or who disguised themselves with a phony voice (pretending *not* to be a regular.) You developed an ear for this.
11. Were old, or (worse) *sounded* old. (I know, that's "ageist." But the ratings war among talk shows demanded that producers targeted a younger audience, like 25 to 54. It was all tied into marketing and advertising.)
12. Used profanity. If any one of those infamous four letter words flew out of a caller's mouth *before* he or she was on-air, then imagine what might happen when nervous and *on* the air. Of course, that's when the dump button came in handy. And that's why every live radio and TV talk show, even those with fully vetted guests, are on a seven- to 15-second delay to this day.

The first dump button I ever encountered was red with a hinged cap on it for quick access. The reason for the cap? So no one accidentally hit it. One newly-hired host wandered into the control room during a break and innocently asked, "What's this for?" not knowing that when he hit it while asking the question, the last seven seconds of the commercial was cut. In other words - two-thousand dollars' worth of airtime disappeared from the planet. We eventually had to run a "make-good," a fully-run commercial, at a later date.

Rules were meant to be broken

Just as I barely gathered all the rules for filtering through callers, Nancy threw me a curve. "The crazy thing," she said, "on any given day, any one of these 'rejects' could fit in perfectly - depending on the host, the news of the day, and the flow of the topics." She must have detected the turn of my stomach because she then followed up with, "Don't worry - you'll develop judgment. But learn fast."

After years in the business, I learned that rules for screening callers varied from show to show. For example, as mentioned earlier, Rush Limbaugh preferred speaking to those who disagreed with him. In fact, the angrier ones were moved to the front of the pack - thus providing Rush with a sparring partner. Larry King pretty much took any caller who had a bent to be entertaining. Sally Jessy Raphael liked quirky career, family, and other social issues - even if she couldn't answer the question. One such example came from a caller in Alaska who asked, "What do I do about a dead horse on my front lawn?" Wanting to entertain, she asked if any listeners had an answer while she asked the caller if it was true that kids in Alaska played outside with miners caps on their heads during the dark months. (The caller, in fact, said that hers did.) Tom and Ray Magliozzi, the legendary hosts of NPR's "Car Talk," actually prepped and recorded each and every caller - and then edited and assembled these mini-theatrical car challenges into hourly blocks.

As time went on and I developed a finer-tuned ear for callers who made the grade, I discovered there was always another gem on the end of a blinking line, that is, if I trolled hard enough. These gems moved to the front of the line to speak to the host - for fear they might have gotten cold feet and hung up. Here are a few memorable ones:

- A blind man whose sight returned for the first time after 25 years.
- The bride-to-be who discovered she was getting married to a brother who grew up in a different orphanage.
- A coal miner who called on a special phone from deep in the earth wanting to propose to his girlfriend - but ended up telling us about what it's like to work hundreds of feet below ground, rarely seeing daylight.
- The woman whose husband had been badgering her for a threesome their entire marriage - and after she finally gave in, she fell in love with the other woman.

There were hundreds more. And, in time, my phone skills had enormous payoffs later in life. (I'm really good at hanging up on telemarketers and cold-calling nearly anyone.) But as with many gigs, you jump one hurdle, then another pops up. Mine came in the form of a headset. With my hands free to screen through callers, Nancy said, "You're ready to multi-task." That was how I came to run the audio on the engineering board. Being an English major in college never covered this skill-set.

I punched through the lines with my left hand and profiled the caller with my left ear, while listening to the live show with my right ear, and running the audio-faders with my right hand. My eyes checked the countdown clocks for when to hit the commercial breaks (left hand) and then occasionally glanced at the host in case he/she was signaling me. All the while, I was ready to hit the "dump button." Did anything ever slide by?

Shit happens

Among my many oversights was when I forgot to turn off the mic during a commercial break on "The Bruce Williams Show." As anyone who had worked with Bruce knew, he was a businessman of extraordinary diversity. (He ran real estate sales, a barbershop, nightclubs, a floral store and a Christmas tree farm - among many other ventures.) He also had a talent for stringing together a few toasty four-letter words behind the scenes. You can get into a mess of trouble with the FCC - you know, the Federal Communications Commission. But on this particular night, we lucked out since no one filed a complaint and only one caller referred to it quickly on air saying, "Whoo-ee Bruce, my ears are still burning!"

Howard Stern is quite another story. Between 1990 and 2004, the "Feds" fined his show $2.5 million for airing allegedly indecent language. Of course, most of his listeners loved it and tuned in just to hear Howard walk the line in and out of "indecency." CBS paid the fines and kept Stern around as *the cost of doing business*. However, not everyone in radio is as valuable to their company as Stern was to CBS in those days.

One of the more challenging in-studio events happened one night during the top-of-the-hour news when most producers and engineers around the country run to the bathroom. I returned with one minute until air and reached for the control room door handle when it came off - right into my hand. The second one fell to the floor on the other side of the door. I was locked out. There was no way to open the door.

The good news? Someone was, in fact, inside the room. The bad news? It was the intern and this was only his second night.

With less than a minute before air, I screamed instructions to him through the empty porthole where the door handles used to be. And somehow with adrenaline racing, we both did it - we made it on air, granted without opening theme music. Eventually, the master engineer showed up with his bag of tricks and got the door off the hinges and me back inside on mine. This was one of the many reminders to expect the unexpected.

Of course, the more I worked on live talk shows over the years - the better I got at dealing with the unexpected, including the many I experienced with Sally Jessy Raphael. That's next...

Chapter Five

SALLY GO 'ROUND THE ROSES

Back in junior high when my friends were writing fan mail to their favorite rock stars such as Eric Clapton, Rod Stewart, and Grace Slick, I shot one out to my favorite radio talk show host, Sally Jessy Raphael. I know, I know... weird, perhaps, for a young teen. But if the kids I hung out with thought this was strange or nerdy, not one ever said so.

Especially when I was the only one among us to get a response. And within two weeks.

The eggshell-colored envelope arrived, imprinted with the local New York radio station's call letters, WMCA, raised in shiny blue font on the upper left hand corner. Inside, on matching notepaper, a hand-written note in big circular script done with a royal blue marker was as happy-looking as the message: "You made my day... my week even! Thank you for being on the other side of the radio...." A smiley face beamed at me from beside the signature, "Sally." It was all so magical. My friends were taken aback, perhaps even jealous.

The scruffy-voiced lady who spouted great wisdom and humor from my parents' kitchen radio (or the clunky transistor in my bedroom) was not just a real human, she was genuine. *Authentic!* She thought enough of a 13-year-old to write back. That simple gesture, though I didn't know it at the time, threw me a lifeline into my future. I still have that note today.

Many years after high school when I landed a gig at NBC Radio Networks and got to "hang out" with the "real deal," I learned some of my best life lessons. Sally's deep-seated philosophies will stay with me forever.

"Sallyisms" I will never forget:

Sometimes, "I don't know" is the best answer

When Sally Jessy Raphael burst onto the NBC Radio Networks back in the Fall of 1982, she introduced a "talk-show-as-group-therapy" style - a format that later emerged on her TV show, "Sally," for which she won two Emmys. The self-described "Dear Abby" of the airwaves tapped into lessons and stories from her real life and connected to the listener. Signed on for the first night of the show were 20 stations. Over the next five years, 300 more.

On the other side of the glass, Sally's regular producer screened through as many as 200 calls an hour in search of a fresh or unusual topic.

"How do I find the courage to tell my parents that I'm gay?"

"I just discovered my husband likes to cross-dress - now, how do I deal with it?"

"Do you think I'm wrong for refusing to go to my daughter's wedding?"

Callers asked how to find courage to change their lives, heal from heartbreak, or triumph over adversity. Often if a producer screened deep enough, something quirky would emerge, like that desperate woman from Alaska who asked, "What do I do about a dead horse on my front lawn?"

Sally's "Wait - WHAT?" response underscored the absurdities that real life threw at each and every one of us. But more surprising than not knowing the answer - was that she admitted it. On the air! Which most hosts would *never* do.

"Someone in the audience will know the answer," she'd say and then invite callers to dial 1-800-TALKNET. (Note: Out of curiosity I called the number the other day and what I got was a sex line.)

From the remote ranches of Wyoming to the hills of western Massachusetts, callers offered explanations. As important as their answers were, the subtext is what made it special... Sally gave the callers a chance to star. And like a friendly neighbor, not a "know-it-all," her door swung open regularly.

Rather than play the role of the credentialed "doctor" or "psychologist," Sally was a throwback to what my husband refers to as the "wise woman in the town square" who people, in simpler times, came to for feedback and advice.

KISS! (Keep it simple, stupid)

Sally had been on the air about three years when I landed the late-night producer shift on "The Neil Myers Show" in the studio a few steps away. She might just as well have been a universe away. The airtight doors were always shut when I would pass by. The lights were so dim I could barely see squat through the sliver of glass on the door. And believe me, I tried. The control room was always "peopled" which became evident whenever the soundproof doors swung open and a roar of laughter exploded out. The show would end, the entourage would file into the hallway and trail Sally out the building, surrounding her like a fence.

While I never had so much as a chance encounter with her at the proverbial water cooler those first few months on the job, I did get my dose of "Sallyisms" every night. I would eavesdrop on her live show, punching up the audio from her studio and funneling it into mine while I went about my producer checklist of chores like erasing old tapes, threading blank ones onto reel-to-reel machines, stacking commercial carts in the order they'll be played, organizing ad copy for the host to record, and testing all the audio components.

This went on for four months. Then one night I got "the call."

Sally's regular producer was out sick and I was designated the substitute. There I sat, a bundle of raw nerves on the other side of the glass from the woman universally recognized as a trailblazer in the industry, and whose response to my fan letter over a decade earlier plotted a path to this very moment. I thought I was going to barf.

I rifled through as many as 100 calls an hour - from teenagers to grandparents, just about the same number of men as women - a mix of trauma-drama-and-emotion, life's highs and lows, all serving up as "entertainment" for listeners across the United States.

Sally got the wackiest calls. In the course of an hour, we heard from that coal miner in Kentucky looking for a creative way to ask his girlfriend to get married; a blind man in Kansas asking how to find a job; and an ex-con imprisoned for rape who was trying to settle into a new life in his old neighborhood.

As I worked the phones, I'd hear bits and pieces of her advice: "Be direct," "Keep it simple," "Dream your dream," "Just do it." These simple, core "Sallyisms" I came to know over the years were flying by me in a brutally fast-paced three hours. My only complaint? I was so busy picking out the next call that I never heard a full sentence during the entire show.

Riding this rollercoaster with the end in sight, I prepped the very last call - Jerry from Plattsburgh, New York. On-air, he followed my directions and launched into his sob story just as we discussed off-air, how his girlfriend dropped him the night before his birthday, and blah-blah-blah-blah-blah. I was sinking into his elaborate tale of woe, while also feeling accomplished for this strong and heartfelt finish, when this Jerry ricocheted into "Baba-Booey – Baba-Booey..." over and over and over again.

Wait – *WHAT?*

Please – NO! Not the "Baba-Booey" caller!

Here's the back-story. This "Baba-Booey" caller, as many producers (and astute listeners) knew, was a regular hoaxer who crank-called talk shows for kicks while ranting the nickname of Howard Stern's well-known producer, Gary Dell'Abate. Most of us in the business figured that he was a disgruntled current or former radio employee because of how precisely he'd time his rant just when we needed to break for a commercial (thus throwing off the exact timing for this network show). In other words, this caller was a *radio terrorist* and I was dead meat.

I already said this but it bears repeating - anyone who's ever screened calls for a living knows you're only as good as your last call. Now, my big night substituting on Sally's show ended with a crash and burn. Sally shot me a glance through the glass... and the next thing I knew I was sitting across her desk in the talent office, out of everyone's earshot. I was about to burn in producers' hell, or so I thought.

"What happened?" she asked.

I paused and heard my inner-Sally chime up from inside my head, *BE DIRECT.* "I screwed up," I answered.

"How?" she shot back.

I paused and thought of another "Sallyism," *KEEP IT SIMPLE.* "I didn't screen the call deep enough," I responded squirming in my seat.

"How do you screen deeper?" she asked, leaning forward.

KEEP IT BRIEF (yes, another one) – at which point I described the two best tricks we producers learned along the way to vet a caller. (Though there's no telling those here, or someone will track me down and assassinate me).

The grilling was over. Just as she told her callers, she kept it simple, direct, and brief. And that's exactly what *I* did. Before long, I was asked to substitute again.

Family is whomever you choose to call family

The first night I substituted on Sally's show, I met the "studio-flies," the regular visitors who swarmed in and around the control room. Meeting and categorizing them was just like a game show: "Quick - for $300, name the 'bloods,' the 'adopted,' the 'fosters,' and all other Sally 'relatives.'"

The correct answers:

- J.J., adopted, 13-years-old at the time and an amazing conversationalist who chattered away even when you wanted silence.

- Allison, an older biological daughter from Sally's first marriage, in her late-20s, a chef and graduate of the School of Culinary Arts.

- Andrea, blood, in her 20s as well, a massage therapist, also from husband #1.

- Karl Soderlund, her second spouse, business manager and advisor, former program director (and present most every night).

- Catherine, foster, from Ireland, who came to visit Sally for a week and stayed three years. (Catherine's older brother Darragh had been in and out of the Raphael household years earlier.)

- Robbie from Puerto Rico, also foster. We producers heard about him, but never met him.

While keeping track of Sally's expansive family life was challenging and a kind of reality show on steroids before such television existed, this much was certain - her "children and family" were a variety pack. In the small gray windowless control room that night, all that mattered was the laughter that filled the time and space.

And that was the norm. They were *family,* Sally's family. Later I learned about others who found their way to Sally's door - a radio colleague who needed a place to stay while settling into this new city, as well as a producer on a tight budget looking for a venue at which to get married (who eventually walked down the aisle at Sally's bed & breakfast in Bucks County, Pennsylvania).

As a result of Sally's range of life experience, the producers knew we could toss her nearly any topic whatsoever - such as a runaway 14-year-old pregnant girl in New Mexico who was debating whether or not to return home, a single father raising two pre-teen daughters asking how to talk to them about S-E-X, or a tortured mom dealing with a child who sleepwalks. Sally even took occasional calls off-the-air, including a memorable one from a teenager who we all thought was suicidal. In this case, the regular producer called the police and had the call traced.

Who is family? In Sally's world, that answer sometimes even extended through the fiber optics to the callers.

So much of the magic in radio is the "theater-of-the-mind"

One night, moments after the "on-air" sign illuminated in the studio, the phone lines died. No phone lines, no callers. No callers, no human interest stories. No show. With that, we had an hour to fill.

The control room transformed into a triage center with techies plugging and unplugging equipment, pulling panels off the walls, turning phone and cable lines into a massive bowl of spaghetti-wires and filaments around us.

Something was desperately wrong and Sally resisted going to our emergency pre-taped segments. These were backups for unexpected moments like this and stashed on the counter within arm's reach.

All you could hope was that it was temporary. Or, that you were working with Sally.

Another broadcaster might have gotten so distracted by all the bodies on the other side of the glass. But Sally just settled back in her chair and yakked. And then she talked some more. We heard about favorite talk shows she listened to when growing up - Arthur Godfrey, Mary Margaret McBride (who hosted a daily woman's advice show), and also "Ma Perkins," a soap opera featuring Ma's homespun philosophies. These voices became cemented into her memory, she said, and served as her early inspiration. Sally and her parents discussed the details of their lives at dinner as if they were regular visitors to the house.

Meanwhile the phones were still dead.

Sally then threaded her story from childhood through to that current day at NBC Radio on the eighth floor of 30 Rockefeller Plaza. She recalled more broadcasters from history who once walked those very hallways.

"You can breathe in the past here - Bob Hope, Jack Benny, Burns and Allen..." and on and on she went, "right in this very building!" She transported us through decades past.

By now, nobody cared that the phone lines were still dead. Sally then peered through the glass at Jimmy the engineer and asked, "Can't you just feel their presence when you're walking down the hall?" Then she did something that no other host back then did - she invited Jimmy the engineer to pop on his microphone and join her on air.

Jimmy, whose overnight shift stretched past 4:00 each morning, responded, "Thanks a lot Sally. Until now, I never thought about ghosts following me around here after you leave for the night."

Sally was all about theater-of-the-mind.

Always opt for good old-fashioned fun

What unfolded in Sally's studio was as fun and engaging as a pajama party. So much of it was unpredictable. And while you can't really say to management, "We were laughing so hard that we missed the commercial break," the truth is circumstances easily came unhinged given, well, all the *fun.* Management was constantly reminding the producers about "the new listener" scanning the dial, tuning in at some random moment just when we positioned a bad call or misfired a commercial which then causes the "dreaded dead air." You never, ever, ever want dead air - especially when you're a fill-in producer. And substitute producers are notoriously balls of nerves anyway.

The challenge: Sally. You just never knew what she might do next to push her wall of creativity. Such as the time when we returned from a commercial break.

Through the talkback and into her earphones, I gave her a 10-second shout. A few breaths later, I whispered, "Five till we're back...," counting her down with my fingers, even though I noticed that she was looking elsewhere and not engaged. Then through the talkback, I announced, "Back!"

I waited. Nothing. Dead air.

Again into the talkback, this time I shouted, "On!" and pointed directly at her. At which point, our eyes locked so I knew she heard me. Or did she?

The mic was hot, the "on-air" sign lit brightly... But still - dead air. Trust me, dead air sounds worse when you're the fill-in producer. The anxiety bug crawled up my back.

"She knows we're back on - right?" I asked Jimmy the engineer who knew her better than most anyone else on staff.

"Don't know," he said, craning his neck, stumped himself.

"How long do I wait until I storm through the glass wall and shout again 'We're back! We're back!'?"

Before Jimmy could answer - we heard something unexpected. A whistle! Sally was whistling and it got louder and louder, until finally she turned to us in the control room and asked, "Oh - are we back?" Then she caught my eye and winked. "I guess I wasn't paying attention."

Theatrical, quirky, fun... and yes, an original.

Sally once philosophized about keeping those of us in the control room guessing what might happen next, because then she would likely do the same for those eavesdropping from home - or the random listener scanning the dial.

How did she acquire that playful attitude?

Of all the broadcasters she listened to while growing up in Scarsdale, New York, she credited Arthur Godfrey for influencing her most. While most 1940s radio announcers were "buttoned up and formal," Godfrey was folksy and real. "From him I learned how to speak in simple declarative sentences," she explained - unlike others who felt they needed to impress listeners with big vocabulary words or complicated ideas.

"It's all about simple, keeping life simple," she'd say on air, "and don't forget to whistle while you work."

Follow your heart and the rest will fall into place

A "Sallyism" was a fortune cookie-sized message - usually a nugget of wisdom that she'd weave into her conversation. Although, I've cited a mere handful, Sally had hundreds. For example...

"Most everyone aims for stability. Yet, it's IN-stability that breeds character."

"Safe doesn't always translate into happiness."

"A lack of certainty tests your imagination."

By the time the 50-something Sally was broadcasting nationally on the NBC Radio Networks in 1982, she had lived a life that reaped great wisdom. By the time she had landed this major gig, she had a sizable broadcasting history - 24 jobs in nearly as many years. She often proudly stated, "...and I was fired from 18 of them." Not all of them were in radio as a talk show host.

She was briefly a correspondent for the Associated Press during an uprising in Santo Domingo. In Puerto Rico, she hosted a television puppet show as well as a cooking show in "Spanglish." For a stretch of time, along with her husband, she ran a restaurant in New York City and, as mentioned earlier, a bed & breakfast in Bucks County, Pennsylvania.

But she always returned to radio, hoping for the Big Payoff. "The only thing that made me happy, that I knew best - was to be a broadcaster," she often said on-air.

"I followed my heart." Even if doing so, on a number of occasions, reaped little more than heartburn.

She often shared a story about leaving a secure job in Miami, which paid her and her husband Karl a combined weekly wage of $250. In search of a bigger salary and a larger market, they packed up the kids and in her typically larger-than-life fashion, drove out of town in a "beat-up Mercedes with nothing but a case of champagne, crackers, and a few bottles of Yoo-Hoo." Without so much as a lead or contact, she and Karl followed their dreams to New York City, only to meet roadblocks.

While she would eventually make it BIG in the Big Apple, this would not be that time. But give up? Not for a second. After multiple rejections in New York City, Sally and Karl landed in nearby Hartford in a gig that paid nearly 50 percent more than the job they left behind in Florida.

As she often recalled on air, "I was never in one place long enough to furnish a home." This time was no different. Her kids and husband lived in the family room "in sleeping bags and ate off the floor" in an old farmhouse they rented in rural Glastonbury, Connecticut. But hey, she had a job. Until, of course, the job fizzled out - which, on her way to the Big Time, was the norm.

In these early years of her career, Sally wound up back in Florida, on to Puerto Rico, then Miami, Ft. Lauderdale, and several stops in between. Along the way, she and her family slept in the car and at one point even lived on food stamps.

Eventually, all the hard work paid off. But it started with a dream and she knew that.

I had married young

Sometimes we learned more about Sally by what she *didn't* say. One such subject? The ex-husband, the Mr. Sally-before-Karl. She never talked about him on-air, she never mentioned him in the studio, and she barely wrote about him in her autobiography *Sally: Unconventional Success* (St. Martin's, 1990). In fact, when it came to Sally's first marriage, most of her producers agreed that this subject was clearly off-limits.

Which of course, only made us more curious... especially since she was so open about many other aspects of her personal life. We microscopically analyzed the brief allusion a mere two-and-a-half pages into her biography where Sally writes, "I had married young." Basically those four words told the beginning-middle-end of her first marriage.

"I knew that our marriage had gone the way of Santa Jesse," she disclosed, in reference to a horse that dropped dead at the finish-line the day that she and her then-husband were visiting the racetrack in Puerto Rico. In nine short paragraphs, it was clear the marriage went hoofs up.

Sally talked plenty on-air about her personal life, except this. It was evident to anyone in the studio - or reading her book - that she followed her heart, married Karl, and went on to live a whirlwind life. They're still together today.

"No matter what happens in our lives, Karl and I instinctively turn the experience into a major motion picture," she said.

Which leads to another Sally philosophy, for which she actually credits Karl...

When all else fails, go shopping

At NBC Radio, producers took phone calls from newly-single moms, suddenly-widowed dads, fresh-from-the-unemployment line construction workers and teachers - every walk of humanity, often teetering between hope and despair.

Each caller, Sally once said, was a character in "a modern day morality play that served as a wake-up call" for listeners also headed down the wrong track. She'd zero in on the heart of the situation, then serve up her own well-earned wisdom. "When all else fails," she'd say, "the best thing you can do is to get up, get dressed, go out of the house… and *go shopping*."

She believed that we humans are our own worst enemy "and must get out of our own way." Another "Sallyism" is, "Move a muscle, change a thought."

She would whisper to a caller, "In my house, when the going gets tough, Karl goes shopping. Being married to him, so goes I." Even when money was tight. At times they'd go to a flea market, an auction or Goodwill with a one- or two-dollar limit. "As if it were a sport, or therapy. It's all about the hunt," she'd add.

Thanks to those bygone days, she has a large collection of eggbeaters, toy trains, or rabbit knick-knacks to remind her, "When the going gets tough, the tough go shopping."

So much of life is how you handle "Plan B"

At NBC Radio's Talknet, Sally opted to do "what I do best - give advice." The "Dear Abby of the Airwaves" zeroed-in on humanity's greatest concerns (according to Sigmund

Freud) - love and money. By 1987, about two years into her successful run with NBC, her affiliate list burgeoned and Sally was a broadcasting sensation – one of a handful of females who achieved this status in the modern era of radio. (Dr. Joy Browne ranks as today's leading advice-giver.)

It was no surprise that Multimedia Television approached her to host her own show - "The Sally Jessy Raphael Show," eventually renamed, "Sally." Unfortunately, it meant she'd commute weekly from New York to St. Louis, some 871 miles each way. To honor her radio contract, which required that she host her nightly three-hour program live, she had to tape five hours of her TV shows within two-and-a-half days - cramming show prep, a parade of guests, and multiple wardrobe changes - while also broadcasting on Monday and Tuesday nights from a remote radio studio in St. Louis. On Wednesday morning after finishing any other television business, she'd fly back to New York to again be live on radio for the remainder of the week. She maintained this grueling schedule for over a year. Listeners never knew she was on remote those first two nights of the week. No doubt, Sally racked up a lot of frequent-flier miles, and the rest is broadcast history with two successful talk shows - the one on TV ran nearly 20 years.

Alas, all good things must come to an end

On page 134 of her autobiography, Sally writes those exact words stated above, followed by, "I was in the midst of contract negotiations with NBC in 1987, and was just about to sign up for another few years, when I was told that NBC had decided to pull out of the radio network business. It had nothing to do with me or the show and everything to do with the temper of the times. The big broadcasting giants were crumbling, and crumbling fast."

Sally was right. Eventually that did happen. However, in looking back over those final years working intermittently with Sally, certain events hinted at her dismay with management before her departure. Being a young producer, I didn't necessarily clearly connect the dots at the time. On the air, Sally was happy and breezy or tuned into seriousness when necessary.

One night during a commercial break, in an outburst of anger, she tossed a stack of six reel-to-reel tapes out the window of the building. They landed on a terrace four floors below (and may still be there today). Maybe this was her way of sending a message to management.

Another night, she refused to read live copy for a commercial that featured a "1-800-love-doctor," insinuating that the "so-called love-doctor" was insulting to her on-air persona. This rebellion cost management thousands of dollars in lost revenue. Regardless, they listened and pulled the spot.

Returning to work one Monday, I discovered Sally was gone. Just like that. She quit. She contacted Maurice Tunick, our former program director and the man who originally brought her to NBC, and offered to work across town with his new talk radio division at ABC.

Whatever actually happened behind the scenes, this much is fact - when Sally left the NBC Radio Networks, management was truly challenged to replace her.

We auditioned a half-dozen newswomen, a well-known psychologist, an astrologist, and even a plucky B-actress whose clothing was studded with so many rhinestones that we were blinded sitting in the control room. Try as each might, no one could fill Sally's high heels. The search continued for months until management finally settled on nationally-syndicated advice columnist, Meg Whitcomb. She had written a few books and exhibited great common sense. On the air, she gave sound advice and wasn't all that bad.

She just wasn't Sally.

I knew we were in trouble the first night. The opening theme music faded, the "on-air" light popped on, and I signaled Meg to start in the usual way - by pointing directly at her from my side of the glass. Instead of a happy, chatty introduction, she froze. Completely perplexed, she stared blankly back at me then glanced over her shoulder to where she imagined I was pointing.

"Hello… Say 'hello,'" I prodded her in the talkback. "Say something, anything. Please."

And she did. Meg was a sweet and soft-spoken woman who really seemed to care and listened closely to her callers. But her advice felt like a recipe from a cookbook. The thinking was good, but the heartbeat and joy were missing. We were never going to recreate the magic in that studio again.

Two years later, the talk division at NBC Radio downsized and moved to Washington, DC, leaving most of us unemployed.

As Sally would say, life is all about change.

"You go to school, you get your master's degree, you study Shakespeare, and you wind up being famous for plastic glasses"

Visit the website ThinkExist.com and you'll find the above quote attributed to Sally Jessy Raphael. The red glasses fast became her trademark as a TV host. She liked "to be expressive with clothing - to use it in a theatrical way as a costume."

Twenty-three years passed before I'd see and talk with Sally again. In 2010, she spoke on a panel at *TALKERS* magazine's New Media Seminar in New York, discussing the topic, "Women in Radio." Honestly, I didn't recognize her at first. This real-life Auntie Mame, who was as strong as she was warm and fuzzy, was now a redhead. A *redhead?* With her trademark red glasses. Here's the point: despite all the time that passed, she not only recognized me, but called me by name - and this was nearly two dozen years and just as many producers later.

But there was something else looming on her face. A sadness that seesawed with anger.

By this time, the 2010-version of Sally had witnessed unexpected pain and tragedies. Not only had her Emmy-award winning TV show folded after nearly two decades, but in 1992, five years after she left radio, her 32-year-old daughter from the first marriage unexpectedly died. Her *People* magazine interview spoke to what I saw that day, "My daughter was a chef, and we don't celebrate holidays now. We go away to countries where they don't have Thanksgiving. Christmas is hard. The anniversary of her death is hard. Her birthday is hard. It's all hard. I know I will never again be really, really happy. I have times when I'm more at peace. But there will always be this pain inside. Nothing makes up for that."

Can't we just end on a positive note?

When you screen calls for a radio show, you treat each hour like a play, carefully orchestrating the beginning, middle, and end. You want to line up as many happy calls as sad, as many men as women, integrate both old and young (ideally aiming for the 18-to-54- year-old island of listeners because that's where the advertisers feel they sell best and most). Ideally. In the perfect hour, you end positively, giving the listeners - the ones you're really playing to - hope and maybe even laughter. So why not end positively here, as well?

Sally the broadcaster was full of contradictions and yet made sense. She was as tough as she was soft. She traveled through life on her own frequency with a charisma that broke through earth's force field - and the world was better for that. She caught wisdom in her sails after surviving many of life's storms and was able to share that with her listeners and viewers.

It was a privilege to cross Sally's path. Today - at 80-plus - she posts/tweets on the internet and produces online interviews. And yes, she still wears her red glasses.

Chapter Six

KING AND I

I landed a part-time job with Larry King's radio show in 1986 because I was in the right place at the right time.

My late shift at NBC Radio Networks where I produced "The Neil Myers Show" ended at 1:00 am and no other talk producer was on the premises.

All that was required? Meet Mr. King in the lobby, escort him to the elevator, guide him down the hall to the nearest empty studio, check mics and audio, and then be prepared to do the same with the big-name parade of guests scheduled for the night. Basically, I was a "handler" for an extra 75 bucks a shift.

At the time, this pre-suspenders-wearing Larry King was one of the most successful radio talk show hosts in the industry. At the height of his show's prominence, he had nearly 500 affiliate stations around the country.

Just the year before, in 1985, he began hosting a nightly TV program on the new cable network called CNN (letters that stood for Cable News Network) and "Larry King Live" was getting some buzz. In addition to television at 9:00 pm... then radio after midnight... he was in contract to write a book. Larry King's career was hot.

And it was this book deal with a New York-based publisher that brought him to the Big Apple four or five days a month to meet with his editor face-to-face. I became his

New York producer/handler, working in coordination with his crew in Washington, DC.

Down the rabbit hole with the talk king

Little did I realize when I signed up with "the King of Talk," I would dive into a world as quirky as what you'd find down Alice's rabbit hole.

Consider these highlights of Larry King's life: Brooklyn-born Lawrence Harvey Zeiger was nine when his dad died and his mother went on welfare. He had been arrested for grand larceny in Miami in 1971 (the charges were dropped months later) and battled a gambling addiction over the years only to evolve into a huge philanthropist later in life.

By the time I was working with him in 1986, he had been married and divorced five times. (Later on, wife #8, Shawn Southwick, joked that she's the only spouse to celebrate a double-digit anniversary with him.) Larry was as much a topic to discuss as the guests who came into the studio.

His DC staff booked the guests, faxed me the show materials, and told me how Larry liked his coffee black with one Sweet'N Low. As the coordinating producer, I doled out the background materials for each live guest, sprang into action should a mic fall off the stand, and made sure everyone had coffee. The show ran live during the overnights. Other than going without much sleep, from my perspective at the time, I had landed a primo gig.

A-tier, B-tier, and not so many C-tier

I'm not the kind of person prone to being star-struck. However, I'd be lying if I didn't admit to having a wide-eyed respect for the magnitude of the "names" coming through that studio door.

After all, that was *Larry King* sitting on the other side of the glass. Not only was I getting paid to open his mic (and get him amped with caffeine), but also to schmooze with the biggest celebs of the day - Bill Cosby, Dan Rather, Tom Brokaw, Dave Letterman, and Geena Davis, just to name a random handful (and, yes, fetch them coffee, too). It was *People* magazine on parade.

What I didn't expect in those early days was to see how someone like veteran actor Danny Aiello was just as "star struck" to be in the same studio with Larry as I. Aiello watched King as if in a trance, never blinking, and never having one sip of the coffee I so skillfully delivered.

Aiello wasn't the only guest who became mildly gaga. When Senate Majority Leader George Mitchell dropped by, he was so flustered that I needed to show him in very simple terms how to position the headset onto his ears and adjust the volume. (And all the while I was thinking, what am *I* doing here messing around with George Mitchell's earlobes - a man who, in 1987, was Deputy President Pro Tempore - potentially five breaths and 10 eardrums away from the presidency!)

Wanna-B-tier

Over the six years I worked with Larry, I met another kind of guest who I came to call the "celebrity-groupie." This was someone who was recognizably famous, but not always top-of-mind. He or she would be perched under Larry's wing, all the while remaining quiet and unannounced to the listeners while Larry was on the air. It seemed to me at the time that these "studio flies" dropped in for career or personal advice, while studying Larry with great intensity. They would unleash oodles of questions during commercial breaks - which, by the way, could last as long as eight minutes. From where I sat on the other side of the glass, I heard startlingly raw exchanges that I came to call "the-talk-show-behind-the-talk-show" that listeners had no clue existed. (Sally had her own version of "studio flies," if you recall.)

Long before the host of MSNBC's "Hardball" landed his own gig on TV, Chris Matthews was one such visitor. At the time, Matthews was a "talking head," a regular political analyst on shows such as "Crossfire" and "Meet the Press." His credentials were impressive with that Inside-the-Beltway sort of intensity in his eyes and always nicely tailored in a navy jacket and paisley tie. At the time, he was the Washington, DC bureau chief for the *San Francisco Examiner*, a former speechwriter for Jimmy Carter, and one-time top aide to Speaker of the House Tip O'Neill.

Years later, in his book "*Now, Let Me Tell You What I Really Think*" (Free Press, 2002), Matthews shared his philosophy for career success: "I think that in order to win the game, you first need a seat at the table." For a portion of the book, he describes how he found a seat with various influential people. Ten years after he sat in the studio with Larry, Matthews was hosting his own program.

Another such visitor was sportscaster Bob Costas, who dropped by multiple times. During commercial breaks, I'd hear snippets of conversations, which in looking back now, I understand must have foreshadowed Costas' failing first marriage. Costas was hosting the sports radio version of a Larry King-esque chat show. Like Chris Matthews, Costas would eventually land his own show (1988-1994) - this one on NBC-TV called "Later with Bob Costas." It drew more on general celebrities than sports figures.

My big moment

Most nights, Larry and his Washington, DC staff packed the house with A-tier guests. Sometimes B-tier. And usually his interviews glided on their own momentum in a "touchy-feely-kissy" style. Unlike the "gotcha" mentality that emerged from hosts who came along later, Larry could - and would - strike up a conversation that you'd more likely have with someone while waiting in line at the movie theater. Nothing confrontational. But hey - A-listers are interesting *in and of themselves.*

Which made one particular interview even more striking because it didn't fit the norm. First, the guest was a "phoner," an author who connected to us by telephone. Second, she was not even a C-tier guest. In fact, I can't even remember her name or book title, though I'll never forget the topic, childhood sexual abuse. *Childhood sexual abuse?* Third, since when does Larry cover a topic like this? Everyone knows he was all about celebrities, pundits, musicians, and politicians, right? So I figured this must have been a favor for a friend.

Whatever. The interview was scheduled to run for (an uncharacteristically long) 15 minutes. And 15-minutes only.

A moment here to reference Larry's often-shared philosophy of conducting an interview: "I don't read the guest's book, so I can experience it along with the listener," he'd often tell journalists who've inquired over the years about his long and successful career. "I ask questions that the listeners may have, based on the fact they haven't read it either. We experience it together."

With that in mind, a producer's job could potentially become challenging. After all, we were charged with keeping the show flowing. And on this particular night with nothing other than the author's name and book title (remember - no internet access yet for a quick search about the subject matter) we were, in a word, *screwed.*

Within 30 seconds of the interview's start, a pained look grew on Larry's face as he squirmed in the chair. I gathered that Larry King had never given the slightest thought to this subject. The conversation that unfolded before me was littered by pauses and intermittent stumbles in thought. And though it was scheduled to be a mere 15 *minutes*, it felt more like 15 *hours*.

Fortunately (as it turned out), years earlier as a writer with the teen magazine *Seventeen*, I had not only covered this topic a half-dozen times, but was also loaded with questions. Here I sat fresh with strict orders from my boss ringing in my head: "If the talent doesn't notice you're sitting there, then you've done your job well. Remember - you're just a facilitator between Larry and his Washington team." In other words, keep your mouth zipped.

The anxiety mounted on both sides of the glass - a flustered Larry King with his guest and me, as I watched this respected interviewer twist and turn. I had never talked into his headset before, especially during a live interview, and barely knew where to locate the mic designated "talkback." I even tried to deliver my suggested talking points to him telepathically. But still, no go.

So finally when I could no longer stand the torture watching him squirm, I leaned in to the talkback mic on my side of the glass, pressed the tiny white Chiclet-sized button and whispered, "At what point when you're dating do you tell someone about your history?"

My heart stopped, my mouth went dry, and our eyes connected. And for a second, I wasn't sure what his reaction would be. Then, he repeated those *exact* words into his mic across 500 stations around the country. An electric charge surged through me. In that moment, I understood this job was not so much about a high and mighty Ivy League education, but, rather, a judgment call you clearly make while sitting in the hot seat - and on no sleep. You can't study for this.

A minute later, the guest was winding up her answer. Larry looked my way. I was one-for-one. I inched into the talkback and tossed another.

"How does a victim overcome such a trauma?"

Once again, those very words shot out the mouth of the "King of Late Night Radio" and I shot a glance over to the clock. Eight minutes remained for the interview and it felt like forever. Nothing like pressure to inspire a brainstorm session. I flung another question, and then another, and then another - each one a shot out of the park. Before you knew it, the segment was over. He said goodbye and we moved seamlessly onto the next hour. Nary a word was spoken.

But it changed me for forever. It was my induction into "the art of the judgment call." My boss called those policies "firm rules." Well, guess what? That night, I learned that rules were sometimes made to be broken. As my program director said to me early on, "If the host says nothing, then you did a good job."

I never used the talkback in that way again with Larry - I never had to. His Peabody Awards, five CableACE Awards and multiple other recognitions spoke to the talent. Larry could connect to his audience and his guest by asking the "every man" question, even with the biggest guests of the era. Take the one addressed to former President Richard Nixon, who came onto Larry's television show in 1990 to talk about his book, *In the Arena: A Memoir of Victory, Defeat and Renewal* (Simon & Schuster, 1990).

"When you drive by the Watergate Hotel," Larry asked the 77-year-old former Commander-in-Chief, "do you ever want to go in and see where it all happened?" (For the record, the answer was "No.")

In Larry's book "*On the Line: The New Road to the White House*" (Harcourt, 1993), he describes his interview style this way: "Our show is more like a town meeting than a news conference. I do not go into an interview as a reporter would, armed with statistics to refute the latest political spin coming out of the White House or Congress. I'm better at drawing people out than explaining policy. I know what I do best - and I've made a pretty good living at it. But because I am not a journalist, I do not always ask the follow-up questions a reporter would ask." In so many ways, he was just a "regular guy" - at least in terms of his on-air approach.

The "Incident"

By the time I was two years into my part-time gig with "LK" (as many of the producers called him when we talked behind the scenes), I noticed that unlike other hosts I had worked with, he'd regularly step out of the studio and into the control room during newsbreaks to schmooze. With us - the producer and engineer. As if we were people. And not just furniture in the control room. Many hosts of far less stature in the business are known to treat their producers like unfeeling robots.

One night during the seven-minute, top-of-the-hour newsbreak as I huddled over my paperwork before the final hour of the show, Larry did the usual and stepped into the control room. What was about to occur made me wish that he *did* treat us like robots!

I looked up, ready to review the upcoming hour's guest, but instead, he leaned in with the stealth and precision of a heat-seeking missile and kissed me - smack on the lips!

It was like a suction cup that has grown in my memory to the size of a plunger. It was a true WTF-moment years before the abbreviation was invented.

I was a 29-year-old wiry producer staring into the beady eyes and thick glasses of a man 23 years older, whom it was my job to respect - and who by this time had been married five times. Stunned, disoriented, and dumbfounded, I pulled away and stared in disbelief. It was a standoff.

This is what confounded me: How could a guy in suspenders who communicates with words for a living, and seemed to have solid basic intelligence and common sense, be so *stupid?* What an ego! If he was interested in the ridiculously risky business of developing a relationship with a female subordinate co-worker, there are so many more civilized ways of doing it. What he *did* could easily be interpreted as an assault.

(Speaking of suspenders, Larry started wearing suspenders in 1987 to hold up his pants after he lost a lot of weight post heart surgery. In December 2010, *Time* magazine reported that he owned an estimated 150 pair - the majority in various combinations of reds and blues... but I digress.)

My incident, of course private and in a dark control room, disclosed a completely different insight into the nature of this so-called king of all-night radio. Was this the same man who regularly spoke with celebrated actors and politicians for hours on end? Was this the guy who could talk to an outrageous character like Marilyn Manson as glibly as Nelson Mandela? What was the disconnect when it came to puckering up and pouncing on an unsuspecting female target? My gut tells me there may be a clue here that relates to the multiple Mrs. LKs. *Ya think?*

Back to The Incident: I did not scream "Lawsuit!" I did not yell "You crazy, lizard-womanizer!" (Oh, I thought it!) If only I cracked up laughing like Mary Richards did when Lou Grant planted his lips on hers. Better yet, I wish I had a snappy line to throw back at him. (But who has that sort of clarity without the help of scriptwriters?)

Immediately after prying my face from his, I stared him back down with my meanest *what the hell are you thinking, you lizard!* look ...and Larry slithered back into the studio, finished up the hour and acted like it never happened. About all I could do was collect myself and be grateful for the glass pane that separated us.

Beyond a few relatives and a handful of trusted friends, I never mentioned The Incident publicly or to anyone within the company. Not until now, more than 20 years after - recognizing that it is hardly the most scandalous thing ever revealed about Larry King. But it does apply to *my* story because from that moment on, it gave me much deeper insight into the potentially enormous difference between the images of our icons in the media and what they are all about in reality.

I worked on that show about four more years and the topic never came up between us. The Incident passed like something creepy that goes bump in the night and never a peep was said. Because nothing like it happened before or after that insane moment, I just chalked it up, back then, to being an uncomfortable encounter with an extreme example of the eccentricities that come with the egos and quirky personalities of big-time talk show hosts, not to mention compulsive, narcissistic womanizers.

How do I view it now? I see it as evidence that mixed in with all his good traits and talents, Larry King is also a bit of a jerk.

Which only gave me pause when I subsequently read about his other escapades. One was told by a female journalist who said that after conducting an interview with Larry for a major magazine, he allegedly threw himself over her and onto the dining room table. Do I believe it? Yep.

King's compulsions

Larry always had new and often bigger romantic news to sow, which I learned straight from the gossip pages of the *New York Post*. Like anyone in New York City-based media in those pre-internet days, my celebrity gossip came straight from *Page Six*. You could say that tabloid was my "show prep."

According to this powerful source, the 58-year-old Larry King was getting married to the 43-year-old Julie Alexander, a manager of a lawyer-recruitment firm in Philadelphia. The details:

- They met at a Washington, DC charity event for former 76ers coach Billy Cunningham.
- He proposed after their first date on August 1, 1989 in Chicago.
- The wedding was scheduled to take place a little more than two months later, October 7, 1989, at a Washington, DC restaurant.

Suddenly, I was scheduled on more and more late shifts to work with Larry who now found reason to be in New York, namely to rendezvous for long weekends with the future Mrs. King.

The first time I met Julie, she was dressed in a tailored navy business suit, blond, friendly, unexpectedly serious and most definitely nice. She often hung out in the control room for a portion of the show before they both headed to the Pierre after the show. My status on the producer-food-chain shot up among Larry's Washington, DC crew because I now had met the future wife #6 and everyone wanted details.

Before long, *Page Six* reported about the wedding, including the bold names of people present: Ted Turner, William F. Buckley Jr., Lynda Carter, and New York Governor Mario Cuomo, among others. Paul Anka performed.

And then, just as expected, these same pages reported "marriage trouble." While it's always smart to question any scandal described on *Page Six*, I grew to believe it reflected the mood I'd encounter in the studio at night. If the gossip pages reported that Larry's marriage was strong, there was a correlation to his mood in the studio that night - he was upbeat and happy. If it related rocky events, tension sparked from the other side of the glass.

Over the next two years, it was up-down, up-down, up-down... until it was kaput.

The *New York Post* reported that the couple separated and Julie had moved out of their Washington home. Larry's lawyer, Mark Barondess, was quoted confirming the latest and added, "All Mr. King wants to say is that they have an 'agreement.' He will have no more comments on his private life or that of Mrs. King." The tabloid added that Alexander couldn't be reached, and her lawyer refused comment.

By May, after a separation, the couple had a much-publicized reunion, with Larry declaring, "This is forever," and Julie adding, "We're together forever."

And they were.

Until they weren't.

Or were they?

More and more, Larry isolated during breaks. He withdrew behind the airtight and soundproof door, shut off his mic, and made phone calls during commercials and the top-of-the-hour news. The vibe was most definitely more tense. I got into a new groove whereby I'd signal him through the talkback to return on-air with a 10-second warning, then counted him in from five, until the mic opened.

Before you knew it, Larry was officially divorced again and wandering down the road looking for Mrs. King #7.

Affairs of the heart

While matters of the romantic heart kept Larry's name in the gossip pages, it was his heart attack that propelled him into the hard news and inspired two *New York Times* best sellers. *Mr. King, You're Having a Heart Attack* (Dell, 1989) was the first of two books that told his amazing recovery story from cardiac arrest. What struck me most in those pages was the account he told about his trip to the emergency room on the morning of February 24, 1987. He called his television producer Tammy Haddad to take him to George Washington Hospital where they were met by his radio producer, Pat Piper.

That told me a lot about this man. Whom you call when you need to rush to the hospital says a lot. Whom you allow to see you in a hospital gown does as well. His peeps were his inner-circle staff. They were his family.

After my job at NBC Radio dissolved in 1993, gone too was my gig with Larry King. I went on to work at CBS Radio Networks and had a few occasions to run into the late-night talker at industry events and of course watched him numerous times on the tube. I even caught a weird "behind-the-scenes" segment on TV which - believe it or not - featured an elaborate hair dye job by a television make-up woman spraying color on the crown of his head where he had a bald spot. I was shocked that he allowed such a private process to be shown on national television. It seems Larry King has a touch of the media-exhibitionist in him. And let us not forget the time he spontaneously kissed Marlon Brando during an interview that will live forever on YouTube. (I guess the legendary actor had his own "incident" with the "Sultan of Smooch.")

Of the three times I ran into him, post-"handler"-job, the most warm and memorable was in October 2011 when he spoke at *TALKERS* magazine's Los Angeles Regional Talkers Forum with an address in which he discussed his career - past, present, and future. The audience of radio broadcasters gave him a standing ovation even before he began to talk. At this point, he had been recently "let go" from his iconic CNN nightly show and was long-retired from radio.

We had a brief conversation over bagels and cream cheese (hundreds donated, by the way, from the Beverly Hills outlet of one of the talk show host's latest business endorsements, nationally-franchised Original Brooklyn Water Bagel Company).

This was when he gave me a quick lowdown: yes, he traded in his microphone for a little league coach hat and watches his kid play ball. He was married (still) to wife (#8) Shawn Southwick, at which point he introduced me to his "father-in-law," a man about Larry's age or younger. I noticed Larry had a little more gray at the temples.

As time went on and I gained even more distance from that colorful chapter and experience in my career, a number of Larry King's ex-wives crossed my path in March 2012 in a theater at Florida Atlantic University in Jupiter, Florida. Well, not exactly. That's where I attended a two-hour, one-woman show titled "The Many Wives of Larry King." (When I saw it listed in the school's bulletin, how could I possibly resist attending?)

Eighty-year-old local Palm Beach County actress Myrna Goldberger transformed herself into the seven wives (eight marriages) of LK, complete with costume changes. It was an amazing piece of work - especially considering that Myrna wrote and performed it herself, having never met Larry King nor his wives! (Check out her website at myrnagoldberger.com). With anecdotes fished directly from Larry's own memoir *My Remarkable Journey* (Weinstein Books, 2009), she *told* his remarkable journey - only as she surmised it would appear if told *through the eyes of his seven wives.*

Clearly, this is the stuff of which novels and movies are made.

Talk show hosts - at least very successful ones - are extremely quirky people. Recognizing that fact and dealing with it is a big part of the foundation of a talk show producer's skill and career.

Storied life experience expressed through an eccentric-but-likeable personality makes an effective talk show host. Larry King fit the bill.

...and *that's* just on the personal front. Seven wives, eight marriages, seven divorces, an annulment, a remarriage, and at least one separation. Slander lawsuits with an ex-wife and then another with an ex-girlfriend. A high school squeeze, a Playboy Bunny, and, of course, an Angie Dickinson. Add to that, an offspring unknown for 30 years.

In case you're curious, Starcasm.net lists all the wives - with photos and brief bios. Check it out if you want names, dates, details and a bit of dirt. It reads like something out of a daytime soap.

I sure learned a number of lessons working with a host like Larry King. Perhaps, at heart, what drives this man is that he just can't get enough - not wives, not hot guests, not TV jobs.

Even after he "left" CNN after 25 years, as a historic broadcasting icon, he stayed on the payroll hosting "specials." But that soon came to an end as well. Eventually, he jumpstarted "Larry King Now" as an online program at Hulu.com. At the time of this writing, he is also doing a nightly political talk show on RT America television, Ora TV, and a weekly podcast with his wife for Podcast One.

Maybe he'll be around forever.

One more thought: In July 2009, I happened to catch Larry King on "The Tonight Show." Sitting across from Conan O'Brien (during his brief tenure), Larry stated that he'd be interested in cryogenics and hoped to be frozen upon death - like celebs Ted Williams and Walt Disney. At this point Conan asked, "What if you wake up in 500 years and don't know anyone?"

True to character, Larry responded, "I'll just make new friends."

Chapter Seven

THE ART OF THE SCHMOOZE

There are Romance languages... and there are GREASE languages. Schmoozing is Grease. It's the one that gets things done in the behind-the-scenes world of booking guests. Producers who work with a host like Larry King need minimal schmooze talent. That's because most wanna-be guests and their handlers will find and schmooze the producer. And superstar-guests almost always have a producer's full attention – and know it.

It was when I worked with lesser-known talents that I needed to exercise my skills in this arena - "Basic Survival Schmooze 101." After all, most potential guests invited on the hundreds of talk shows around the country have not necessarily heard of the hosts (or their producers) inviting them.

To be an effective producer requires "people skills." If you can schmooze with the best of them, contacts will be less likely to question the size of your audience.

There was more to this job than just booking celebrities (usually promoting something). There was inexplicable joy in yanking a gem of a guest out of nowhere - the unexpected someone that no other producer had yet to book, or was even thinking of booking - a "no-name" at the center of a big story (or significantly connected to it) that hadn't shown up as a player on the topic's front page coverage, had no publicist (yet), and was a yapper of enormous intelligence and authenticity. A *natural.* This type of potential guest *also* required schmooze because they had no vested interest in coming on the show (i.e. they were not "plugging" anything) and were potentially what is referred to in the business as a "newsmaker."

The saga of David Koresh's girlfriend

One of my most memorable "gets?" A former girlfriend of David Koresh, the Waco, Texas cult leader. As you recall, Koresh claimed to be a prophet of the Branch Davidian religious sect who - along with 76 of his members (including 17 children under 17) - died on April 19, 1993 in a fire that resulted from a controversial siege by the FBI.

Had the stand-off not continued for 51 days, I might never have landed my guest. But the story grew in unexpected directions and the public was gripped by a marathon of daily headlines such as "Latest with wack-o in Waco" or "It's getting wackier in Waco." Talk radio, of course, was eating it all up.

As the days mounted, so did the quirky ambush techniques that negotiators used in hopes to force the Davidians to surrender from the Mount Carmel compound. They shined bright lights through windows all night, blasted a range of loud esoteric music such as Tibetan Buddhist chants, Alice Cooper, and bagpipe solos. They followed that with the nerve-shattering sound of dentist drills.

The media "went circus" on this story. Talk shows such as the one I produced asked callers to suggest songs they felt could bulldoze the hostages out of the Branch Davidian's encampment. For 51 days, we covered this story endlessly, booking religion experts, former cult members, even neighbors who knew Koresh when he was a child.

And then a mega-lead came in through an unexpected channel.

A few nights before the Koresh ranch burned down, my friend Catherine from LA called me at home with her latest adventures through the Midwest while visiting her brother. She mentioned, in passing, that her brother's childhood friend was recounting how he dated a woman who once dated David Koresh. My heart stopped. Through this connection, I calculated I was a mere four-degrees of separation from Koresh.

With Catherine, I never had to schmooze - we were way beyond that. I asked her for the brother's phone number and contacted him immediately, requesting that he call his friend to grease my introduction. I schmoozed him to schmooze his friend.

An hour later, I was talking to the friend. That was where it got challenging. First, I learned that he hadn't actually spoken to Koresh's ex for quite a while. "Maybe over a year," he muttered. But he was still willing to give it a try. That is, if he could "find her number."

Uh oh, all of a sudden, this was not looking so great. However, two days later, when I assumed that any prospects for getting the girlfriend's number were dead, the call from the friend-of-the-friend-of-the-brother came in. He found the phone number! But the slightly bad news - he did not grease the introduction. For that, I was on my own.

When it came to cold-calling people I didn't know, I was fearless. I learned that people loved to talk - and if you could hit them up just right, that is *schmooze,* they'd spill everything.

The girlfriend answered the phone. I got her! Or at least I got her on the phone...

I introduced myself, dangled my CBS affiliation at the top of the conversation and then launched my usual opening line:

"You probably don't get a call like this every day," I began. "So allow me to introduce myself..."

I was always shocked, elated really, when the person I hoped to reach actually picked up the phone. I never took that for granted. Secondly, I've often been amazed - after I explained why I'm calling - that my intended guest did not hang up after bombarding me with a nasty name or two. (Though that has happened as well.)

I admit that what I did for a living was sometimes dirty and exploitive, or easily interpreted that way. And until I had gotten yelled at by an unfortunate victim of the Colin Ferguson Long Island Railroad shooting, I hadn't really thought about the psychological trespassing I occasionally committed. I had truly believed that what I did day-to-day *was* investigative and informative and therefore in the interest of the greater good. Or, I wanted to think so. Today, my thinking is quite different.

Back to David Koresh's ex-girlfriend. The "pre-interview" checked out. She really did have a history with the shaggy-haired, self-proclaimed prophet. And the second most amazing thing - she agreed to come on the air *that very night.*

We hung up and for the next 10 hours, I was so filled with anxiety that I broke out in hives. I was living every producer's nightmare. I found a gem of a guest, created in-depth talking points after an extensive pre-interview, cleared the decks (canceled decent talking heads who would never come on again out of vengeance), and now I was living in fear that some scavenger in television will sniff me out and hijack my prey... er, I mean my guest. It happened all the time.

Here's the deal. Talk show producers have a sixth-sense about these things. I could meet a fellow producer at the elevator or the commissary, and she could tell something was up. She'd *smell* it. And at CBS, I was surrounded by high-flying pros hammering out their guest list for such shows as "60 Minutes," "48 Hours," you name it. They didn't land those jobs by being Little Mary Sunshine.

Add to this, I worked in *radio*, meaning, small budget (zero). Television producers' goodie bags are so "tricked out" they can (and will) easily kidnap a guest. A first-class flight to New York City? Easy! Two or three nights at The Ritz? Done! A daily stipend to shop on Fifth Avenue? Sure! Not that I could blame a guest for "cashing in."

So what did I do to protect and nest my guest? Once again, I *schmoozed*. Every two or three hours, I'd call to see if Koresh's former flame had any further questions and followed it up with small talk. In reality, I was checking in. When working an important story such as this one, I'd normally book a back-up guest, just in case the original flickered out. But let's face it, how many David Koresh ex-girlfriends did I know?

Fast forward to the night of the interview: the girlfriend was off-the-charts sensational, she relayed some of the strangest stories about David Koresh, including how - on one memorable date - he rolled down his car window to scream out sermons to passersby. On another night on the town, he tooled around on his guitar, rambling memorized scripture. The tabloids may have owned remarkable headlines for weeks - but that night our radio show featured a most engaging guest.

Sharing the wealth

The proof came immediately - phone calls flooded my voicemail. Morning show producers, bookers and print journalists from all over the country ambushed me for contact information. Reuters, NBC News, "CBS Evening News," NPR, "Good Morning America" and many more tracked me down to get a piece of this new guest pie. In case you hadn't noticed, much of what happens in the media is a game of follow-the-leader.

"The ex-girlfriend" was definitely hot property and when the word got out, requests kept pouring in for days. Everyone who was anyone was interested. And in my world, producers often will share info, *after* the fact. But first, I had an important detail to oversee.

I called the ex-girlfriend. First, I thanked her for her time the night before. Next, I described the tsunami of calls I received and asked if she'd mind if I passed along her number. She did not (boy, was she green). I warned her that her life would be thrown into an upheaval. I also suggested that she call me back should she change her mind... which she did within 24 hours. She not only changed her mind, but her phone number as well.

It was a segment like this that helped take my schmooze skills up a notch. But of course, schmoozing can only take you so far. Ultimately, you better have good content, and frankly, be ready for anything.

Schmoozing is certainly not everything - but it is an important piece of the puzzle.

Chapter Eight

GIL WHO?

One of the more surprising phenomena that I observed working at the CBS Broadcast Center in New York was how easy it was for my particular broadcast unit - made up of a radio host, executive producer, and me - to remain invisible, while *in full view,* from our co-workers. From 1992 through 1994, I was an associate producer booking guests for an award-winning radio newsman/talk show host who was not only successful by industry standards, but well-respected as well for his solid talent and integrity. Gil Gross was, as they say in the business, "a real pro," having accumulated over 100 affiliates around the country by the time I landed my gig.

However, even though he was a major host on a big-time platform, he was basically unknown in the CBS universe.

Hiding in plain sight

For example, it was April 1993 and I had just stepped inside the ladies' room on the sixth floor of the CBS Broadcast Center. A petite woman in a navy suit and silky white collar said hello to me. Her manner was so schmoozy, and in of all places, the bathroom, that I was momentarily taken aback.

"Hi. My name's Connie Chung," she said, stretching out her right arm fully to shake my hand. My producer brain flashed on the factoids - married to Maury Povich, most recently signed a three-year contract at CBS for six-million dollars to host "Eye to Eye with Connie Chung" and a new weekend news show, "Saturday Night with Connie Chung," and had spent years at NBC as a news correspondent.

At which point she asked "The Question." (Now, pay attention - this is the part I was referring to above.)

"So what is it that *you* do here at CBS?"

I had been working at the company for nearly two years and at this point was used to this recurring inquiry. It was a small-town-question in a big-town-place - the type of question people ask to get to know you better.

I took a breath, then responded, "I'm an associate producer for the Gil Gross radio show."

Predictably, my answer was met by a scrunched-nose stare. Also predictably, she followed up with QUESTIONS TWO and THREE:

"There's a radio division... *in this building*?" (Nose still scrunched.) "And who? *Gil Gross?*"

Here we go again, I thought. Most people at CBS were surprised to hear that an actual radio division (let alone a studio - make that *12* studios!) existed in the very building which housed "CBS This Morning," "48 Hours," and soap operas galore. At the time, Bill Maher's "Politically Incorrect" taped there as well, before moving to CBS Television City in Los Angeles.

In moments like this, I wanted to say, "The company you work for - the Columbia Broadcasting System - made its first foray into broadcasting thanks to *radio!* To be exact, that was at 3:00 pm Eastern Standard Time on September 18, 1927. Radio was what kick-started this company and *your current career* into existence. Once upon a time, it even featured its own 22-piece symphony orchestra. Yes, all this on *radio*. All. On. Radio. And big-time successful in its day was the 'CBS Radio Mystery Theater.' I know you've heard of that - which by the way, all 1399 episodes are currently online..."

But to my new friend Connie, I didn't say any of that. Instead, I cheerily pointed out directions to the location of the radio studios, saying, "After you walk through the front door, make the first and immediate right around the reception desk, and you'll find your way there." Not that she was going to.

I skipped the details about the long, dusty hallways that snaked left, and left, and left again into a maze of offices and studios with additional turns and forks. And not one window. Not anywhere. Clearly this isolated part of the building was meant to house a witch's coven.

I strategized that explaining the location to someone like Connie, I may get a pay-off one day. Maybe if a guest bails out at the last minute and I desperately need a replacement, Connie will be the one I can call. And all because we schmoozed in the bathroom.

What did I learn from having been posed "THE QUESTION" over and over again, this time by Connie? Most CBS employees didn't know squat about the radio division, much less Gil Gross... though both were hiding in plain sight. Well... maybe as I look back - in *not* so plain sight. It seems, in the scheme of things at the CBS Broadcast Center, radio was *not* the center of the world and hadn't been for years.

Even Dan Rather, the anchor and managing editor of "CBS Evening News" for 24 years, was rarely, if ever, seen in that area of the building. And in his case, this was even more unfortunate since he contributed nightly to CBS News

Radio. Since March 9, 1981, his daily news analysis "Dan Rather Reporting" was carried by hundreds of radio stations around the country. But come downstairs? Never. He simply linked up with the first floor studio from his second floor desk via ISDN, a digital phone line that transmits studio quality sound via a microphone set up on his desk. Strangely, I bumped into him regularly on the elevator and he never knew that I was often in the studio when he was giving his feed. As pushy as I could be in booking a guest, it was not in my nature to make "hallway" conversation with CBS royalty unless spoken to first (except for an occasional "hello" when passing the gold-plated etching of Edward R. Murrow hanging in the lobby).

Big-time noisy place

Moments like the one in the bathroom with Connie or with Dan on the way out of the building were great reminders of my place in the CBS galaxy. There were opportunities galore to bump into fellow CBS citizenry and I'm not just talking about producers. All I simply needed to do was walk through the revolving front door of the midtown-Manhattan building on 57th Street and I found myself in a living, breathing hall of fame. On any given day, I would be treated to major-league celebrity sightings - William Shatner, Al Gore, Gene Simmons, Brooke Shields, Tonya Harding, or the Reverend Jesse Jackson seated in the lobby, waiting for an intern or a producer to escort them upstairs to an interview.

The funny thing was the phenomenon of stars ogling stars. The celebrities waiting in the lobby seemed interested in sighting the CBS employees who were themselves stars. Leslie Stahl, Steve Kroft, Deborah Norville, or John Roberts, just to name a handful, emerged from black smoky-windowed sedans, dropped off at the front door and in some of these cases, were also subjects of photographic portraits hanging on walls throughout the building.

Meantime, distinguished radio stalwart, Gil Gross, had no driver. His photo was not on any observable wall in the joint - and that included in his own office - even though he had numerous Kodak moments in an admirable career that included interviewing the likes of Bill Clinton and Margaret Thatcher. On paper, he had all the goods - a great on-air presence, a quick wit, and an encyclopedic memory. At 23-years-old, he was the youngest anchorman ever on the ABC Radio Network, an accomplishment that would be on his resume throughout his career. Gil had won multiple awards for his coverage of the attempted assassination of Pope John Paul II as well as the intifada in Jerusalem. He even had the "chops" to fill-in for the likes of Charles Osgood and Paul Harvey on their respective radio shows. His television appearances included "Good Morning America," CNN, Fox News Channel, "America's Talking," "The Week in Review," "The CBS News with Dan Rather," "Up to the Minute," and so much more. In other words, wow!

Despite his award-winning credentials and well-noted intelligence, Gil, and often radio itself, remained invisible and off the radar - even to fellow CBS employees, let alone the general public. Why do some talents as Gil fall short of more widespread recognition? That is a nuanced question that bedevils many in the industry while being clear to others. Part of it was - and still is - due to the lower rung radio occupies, compared to television, in the world of American corporate media - a disparity made more evident at CBS because both divisions were housed in the same large building. But it goes deeper than that and is far more complex. Gil Gross was a case study in the question of what separates a journeyman from a star.

A true celebrity talker

Take a look at another one-time CBS employee, often described as a "shock jock," and the self-proclaimed "King of All Media." Regardless of his choice of subjects and interviews, Howard Stern managed to hone a meteoric successful career - in and outside his radio studio - and become a true household name in his own right.

September 1, 1995 is a good example. New Yorkers woke up to this screaming front page headline in the *New York Daily News*: "PAY UP." The three-inch bold font introduced a story about how Howard's bosses, the owners of radio stations that carried "The Howard Stern Show," had to shell out an eyebrow-raising $1.7-million for yet another episode of dirty-talk banter. *$1.7 million?* Let's face it - if you weren't a listener the day before that headline, you may want to tune in now, just out of curiosity.

Talk about a bullhorn from the newsstand. Howard, by the way, holds the record for being the most-fined radio talk show host by the FCC - a total of $2.4-million by the late-1990s. To quote the biography written by Paul Colford, *Howard Stern, King of All Media: The Unauthorized Biography* (St. Martin's Press, 1996), "You may love him, you may hate him, you can't ignore him."

Why did CBS put up with paying these fines? It surely wasn't for love of the art. Industry insiders almost unanimously explain, "It was simply the cost of doing business." Stern was *that* valuable (at least in that era) to CBS.

Is that celebrity? It clearly was what worked for Howard.

Meanwhile Gil, an award-winning newscaster, was easy to overlook because he, well, was "just" a good doobie and blended in. Now don't get me wrong, that is not necessarily a bad thing. But in the world of mega-egos and huge disparities between the salaries of some performers and the salaries of others - who, on paper, all do basically the same thing - there is a distinct pecking order that is not easily defined by job description, dependability or seniority. Welcome to show business where not all stars shine with the same order of magnitude.

What *does* it take?

What makes some on-air talents big-time celebrities and household names while others - though competent, even award-winning - remain just voices and names on the radio?

Do you have to be dirty? Controversial? Scandal-ridden? Perhaps. But not always and not entirely. Sally Jessy Raphael wasn't any of these things. Yet she was, indeed, a star.

Do you have to be singularly responsible for the ratings and the revenue generated by your show or time slot and recognized by your employers as such? In other words, must you be worthy of the most magic adjective with which a talent can be dubbed - *indispensable*? Now, we are in the ballpark. But exactly what makes a host or radio performer indispensable? It is the loyal legion of fans that make an appointment to listen to *that particular host* every day and tell their friends about what they heard the day before. It is also the large pool of advertisers that believe their businesses are significantly enhanced by being associated with *that particular host* and are willing to pay large sums for a personal product endorsement.

But what exactly are the qualities that make one talent a Howard or a Sally and another a "Gil *who?*" when they are all damn good at practicing the art of radio? How do you recognize and measure the intangibles that constitute likability, charisma and magnetism? How do you teach the "X Factor?"

This is an aspect of the radio business that makes it as much, if not more, an art than a science.

Of course, we mustn't forget about the growing role of sensationalism in popular media. Maybe we were just a little too tame on "The Gil Gross Show." The toughest topics we'd cover, for example included: Should the Pete Rose gambling scandal keep him out of Cooperstown? Should a guy who killed his girlfriend's dog serve time in prison? While producers on Gil's show debated moral issues such as these - a 1990s popular format - a growing number of shows around the country were firing up their own headline stories, ones that landed them in trouble with the FCC as well as special-interest groups - and with that, huge ratings. Some of the more outlandish "segments" came along later, as in these examples from other shows:

- Bubba the Love Sponge had a pig castrated and killed on the air and yes, was charged with animal cruelty (February 27, 2001).

- Opie and Anthony sponsored a contest asking listeners to have sex in a public place - the winners found their way to St. Patrick's Cathedral (August 16, 2002).

My bread-and-butter topics with Gil Gross were hardly as gruesome, yet we had an audience and we had a mission. And so what if those other shows may have beaten us in the ratings? (Well, maybe I *did* care about that...)

Regardless, we were in the game and it made for great conversation.

Except I admit, when it came to those stories that went on and on and on - the ones that just wouldn't go away. Coming up next.

Chapter Nine

STORIES AND GUESTS THAT JUST WOULDN'T GO AWAY

There were stories, and then there were *stories.*

When you work in news/talk radio and TV, the chewy, caloric, fast-foods for a show's content are the people involved in the "can-you-believe-it?" scandals. They were, of course, the ones that helped keep the format mass appeal. Eventually, however, they also taxed my patience. Dave Holloway searching for his missing daughter Natalee after she vanished in Aruba; Lorena Bobbitt, who severed her husband John's "male member," inadvertently contributing the verb "bobbitt" to the lexicon; or the disturbing Michael Jackson child molestation trial. The list goes on.

What's amazing to most news producers and media watchers is that, just when you thought the end was near and you had exhausted all the angles to a story, another wrinkle unfolded and it would twist and take off again. Here are a few gems that just would not go away:

O.J. Simpson

Behold the Ford Bronco. Ever since June 17, 1994, talk show producers from around the country genuflect before the Ford Bronco to honor the sacred story of O. J. Simpson and his famous car chase in Los Angeles on California's Interstate 405 witnessed by over 100 million television viewers. The story made global headlines and triggered a frenzy for TV courtroom dramas. It also carried most of us through the news doldrums of August. Every producer knows how difficult it is to drum up guests and topics during that time of year when so many experts and guests are on vacation.

Lasting 133 days, this celebrity trial spawned more TV shows, careers and best-selling books than any other.

Prosecutor Marcia Clark became special correspondent for "Entertainment Tonight."

Greta Van Susteren, a CNN legal analyst during the trial, soon landed on "Burden of Proof" and "The Point" (before heading over to FOX News Channel where she hosts "On the Record").

Bleach blond O.J. Simpson "houseguest" Kato Kaelin got various one-shot TV roles on such shows as "MADtv" as well as numerous reality shows ("House Guest" and "Gimme My Reality Show" where C-list celebrities competed for their own television gig).

Even the daughters of defense lawyer (and longtime O.J. friend) Bob Kardashian parlayed their dad's household name into a fortune via the reality show "Keeping Up with the Kardashians."

And there were plenty more celebs spawned by the O.J. trial. Talk about a story with legs.

Joey Buttafuoco

What made the Joey Buttafuoco/Amy Fisher story so compelling? Let me count the ways. For one, start with the last name of the owner of the Long Island car repair shop, thank you Merriam-Webster:

Buttafuoco (n.; Italian); 'butta' from the verb 'buttare' to throw, discard; 'fuoco' fire. **Buttafuoco** means to emit flames, possibly a name for a lamplighter in the pre-electricity days.

In addition to the tidal wave of near-mispronunciations, the story ushered a curious public into a most unimaginable world. On May 19, 1992, Amy Fisher (aka, the "Long Island Lolita") shot Joey's wife, Mary Jo, in the head - where the bullet is still precariously lodged to this day. The 17-year-old Amy began a six-year affair with Joey after showing up at his shop in need of car repairs. Convicted of first-degree aggravated assault, she served six years in prison.

Just when we thought we'd never hear about her again, Amy left prison, got married, had three kids and somehow became an advice columnist for the now-defunct *Long Island Press*. Shortly thereafter, her book, *If I Knew Then* (iUniverse, 2004), was published and inspired an ABC television movie starring Drew Barrymore. But that's not all. Somewhere in that timeline, she became a porn actress and - according to the tabloids - she even moved in with Joey. You can't make this stuff up.

By March 2008, Fisher became a commentator on truTV's "The Smoking Gun Presents: World's Dumbest," a series that depicted people caught saying crazy things or doing crazy acts. She and Joey Buttafuoco were in talks to star together in a reality show. Although that never materialized, Amy became a regular on "The Howard Stern Show," as well as an occasional guest or topic on "The Gil Gross Show," and later released a pay-per-view adult film titled "Amy Fisher: Totally Nude & Exposed." (Just for the record, she was the subject of five movies – three made-for-TV and two X-rated.)

Audiences last saw Amy on "Celebrity Rehab with Dr. Drew."

Need I say more?

Michael Schiavo

Between 2005 and 2006, at least eight books were published about the highly-publicized case of Terri Schiavo, the Florida woman in a vegetative state for seven years after collapsing in her home from cardiac arrest. Her husband Michael began a legal (and media) battle with her parents - he wanted to terminate her life-support, arguing Terri was brain dead and kept alive solely with help from a ventilator system; her parents wanted to keep her on life-support, arguing that she was conscious. The husband and the parents authored separate books.

The one that made it to the top of my stack - because it topped off on the polls of public opinion - was written by Michael, the husband, called *Terri: The Truth* (Dutton, 2006). As a producer, one of my jobs was to weigh out the cultural consensus of the public, otherwise known as the court of public opinion. And from where I sat, the public (at least that week) supported the husband.

Michael, however, was not an easy, slam-bam-booking. He demanded his own conditions before agreeing to join us in studio.

I had to promise that he'd be the only guest in studio and no other guest on this topic could join us the hour before, the hour during, or the hour after.

"This is not an experience I wish to debate," he emphatically said over the phone. "I just want the freedom to tell my side of the story without interruption." He actually was quite media savvy.

I kept that promise - and many more. My word as the producer was all I had. It did not take long to learn that certain guests personally invested in sensitive news stories simply wanted the chance to be understood. They were there to tell their truths and sometimes didn't care to know yours.

Joey, Amy, O.J. and the like were a blessing and a curse. These noted persons along with others of their ilk clearly kept the engine of generalist talk radio running. Quite often, only on fumes as the media squeezed every last molecule of interest out of them.

Chapter Ten

BOWTIES AND POETRY

Charles Osgood could regularly be found at his desk at the CBS Broadcast Center before dawn, sometimes before 4:00 am, prepping radio's "Osgood Files" - his live, four-times-daily morning commentaries. That's a schedule he kept since 1971 when the feature first began. On Sundays, radio fans could actually see the man behind the voice on "CBS Sunday Morning," a program he began anchoring in 1994. Before signing off that television gig each week, the man with the trademark bowtie gave a nod to his radio fans, saying, "Until then, I'll see you on the radio."

Mention the name Charles Osgood inside the hallowed halls of CBS and you'd hear him described by the nickname, "poet-in-residence," inspired by his sometimes whimsical, rhyming daily vignettes. Dan Rather called him "a national treasure." Osgood's "Sunday Morning" predecessor, Charles Kuralt, said he was "one of the last great broadcast writers." Former news anchor for "PBS NewsHour" Jim Lehrer described him as "a special mind and voice in a business where his kind is rare."

As if those stamps of approval were not enough, in 1990, Osgood's colleagues nominated him into the radio division of the National Association of Broadcasters Hall of Fame and, over the years, he's been the recipient of (among others) two Peabody Awards, the Marconi Award, and the Radio Mercury Award.

Despite all the accolades, those of us who worked in-studio with him called him "Charlie" - which is exactly how he introduced himself the first day we met when I was ushered to my desk in a windowless office directly across the hall. While I'd show up at 9:00 am for the start of my day with "The Gil Gross Show" (I know - Gil *who?*), he and his staff were winding down theirs and soon gone. Traditional work hours were never part of his then-two-decades-plus career. (Today, he has clocked over four decades on that wacky schedule.) And it was because of his quirky hours that my workday sometimes crossed over with his.

But first let's revisit the climate in New York City in the year 1993.

Five months before I started working at CBS - February, 1993 - a bomb exploded in the basement garage of the World Trade Center, killing six people. The event, which foreshadowed the 9/11 attacks, inspired companies like CBS to ramp-up their security strategies - installing metal detectors in the lobby, multiple cameras outside the building and double-plated, bulletproof glass doors at the entrance.

Photographed for a company ID on my first day as a CBS employee, I was awestruck by the new security system in the sub-basement of the building. It was the only time I ever descended to that subterranean level, an area that looked more like a military command headquarters than a broadcast center. Multiple TV screens on walls flashed on various entrances to the building every four seconds or so - 57th Street, the lobby, then 56th Street, the rooftop, the back-of-building delivery entrance, the soap opera entrance. Panels of lights blinked white-green-yellow-red. A large conveyor belt moved packages along through a machine, no doubt x-raying the contents, much like you see at the airport. Everything that came into the building was inspected. As it turned out, so too were unclaimed items left behind in the commissary, lobby, barber shop, newsstand, you name it.

Which brings me back to my first week at my new job, manning the producer desk for "The Gil Gross Show" across the hall from Charlie. Since Charlie was gone during traditional work hours, I often responded to random Osgood office business - such as signing for FedEx packages. On this one particular morning, a pair of security guards appeared at my office door.

"Notice any suspicious persons on the floor today?" one asked.

"Uh, no," I answered.

"What about roaming outside the men's room?"

I shook my head no, wondering what the heck *this* was all about.

A briefcase, it turned out, was found inside the men's room and nobody on the floor had claimed it. So now a bomb crew would be called to remove and transport it to the security department. All day long, the talk over bathroom stalls and at the elevator bank was on the potential explosive found in the john. By day's end, those of us on the sixth floor conjured up visions of our friendly neighborhood deli-delivery guy as culprit.

Until, of course, the truth was exposed. That unclaimed threatening object belonged to Charlie, the giant of broadcasting. Furthermore, I'd soon discover, that this would be the first of many items Charlie would absent-mindedly leave behind in that clichéd, professorial way. We're talking house keys, an American Express credit card, a winter coat, gloves - you name it. Even his navy Town Car went missing for four days because he completely forgot he had driven in from New Jersey earlier in the week. After his staff and I fanned out in the neighborhood, we found it five blocks away tagged with multiple orange tickets.

Eventually, I evolved into the designated go-to person for lost items that belonged to Charlie Osgood. Worth noting, other treasures never unearthed included his anniversary cufflinks, a few pairs of lost reading glasses, and a money clip. Perhaps they'll unexpectedly turn up one day - much like the famous in-house CBS story about the cow hoof.

When the cows come home

In May 2001, almost 50 years after William Paley's Columbia Broadcasting System moved from Grand Central Station to its current location on West 57th Street in New York, a crew from "48 Hours" explored the musty basement of the Broadcast Center in search of a fresh location for a story shoot. In addition to exposed un-paneled walls, props for soap operas, a carpentry area, and large packing equipment, they discovered remnants from the Sheffield Farms Company, the original and previous occupants of the sprawling building. Yes, what was now CBS used to house hundreds of cows and pasteurization machines, churning up billions of gallons of milk per year.

Fast forward a half-century later, the "48 Hours" crew became the talk at the elevator bank as well as editorial meetings for this delightful nugget of news: they had uncovered dozens of grain chutes as well as a cow hoof. It all became part of the lore employees told visitors to the building.

No doubt, some future archaeological team will excavate the sixth floor and maybe dredge up the still-lost treasures of Charles Osgood. Much like the famous "hoof" story, Charlie's recovered riches will add more color to that mystical land called CBS.

A gathering storm

While I bonded with Charlie and his staff over the lost-and-found items during those early months, what drew us all closer was a mega-snowstorm barreling toward New York City in the winter of 1993/94. Overnight, I went from "search and rescue" to an unofficial fill-in engineer/producer. Believe me - it was not for any talent that I may have possessed, but rather for geography. I lived five blocks from CBS' 57th Street location while everyone else on Charlie's staff commuted from New Jersey or Long Island. Thanks to a five-minute walking commute, I could add a gem to my resume.

Unique, powerful, artistic news programming

"The Osgood Files" focused on a single story whether from the national headlines or an offbeat human interest piece. They were usually topical and news-driven. If you asked Charlie to explain what makes up "The Osgood Files," he'd say something like, "It has to have an element of drama, maybe a twist or surprise. It's got to have characters in it... and you must be able to succinctly talk about them all within two-and-a-half minutes."

If you asked me, a newly trained fill-in producer, that same question, I'd say, "It's the fastest four minutes of my life where every second counts and it's the closest I'd ever come to having a heart attack while producing a show. First you record Charlie's 30-second intro, then the two-minute belly of the story, which included actualities (those eight- to 10-second pre-recorded sound bites by experts or men-on-the-street), and then add the commercials. Oh yes, important: it's LIVE on 350 stations around the country, so you can't screw up. It's a workout crammed into 150 seconds."

A further test for any producer-engineer is working with Charlie on remotes. For 10 weeks out of the year, he actually broadcasted from his vacation home in St. Tropez, France - a convenient location when you considered that the time zone there meant his early-morning live deadlines back in the States were six hours ahead in France. When abroad, he was actually on a mainstream schedule - up with the sun, commuting from the bedroom to his home studio. It just so happened he was thousands of miles away.

I did have the opportunity to work in the New York studio (before 4:00 am Eastern) while Charlie sat at his mic some 5,000 miles away at 10:00 am local time in France. We were connected by "ISDN," the special fiber-optic line that brought us a crisp digital audio, making Charlie sound as if he were sitting on the other side of the glass instead of the Atlantic Ocean. Except, of course, when "désastre" struck.

And sure enough it did. *Fa-boom!*

"What was *THAT*?" I asked one morning.

"The wall," Charlie answered through the talkback.

"What wall?" I asked, never having seen this home studio in France.

"...of the studio. It just fell over."

This so-called wall, I was told, was rigged together with a few inflatable pool lounge chairs and numerous towels, among other items. And though I never actually saw this makeshift studio in person, nor in photos, I did, of course, see it in my mind.

To quote one of Charlie's most popular verses:

No television set that's made, no screen that you can find,
Can compare with that of radio, the theater of the mind...
The colors are more colorful, the reds and greens and blues...
And more vivid yet more subtle than television's hues...

Charlie Osgood knew the power of the imagination. And if you worked with him, you would too. Little wonder he was asked to narrate the Dr. Seuss animated film, "Horton Hears a Who!" (2008).

Before long, CBS Talk Radio was expanding and management offered me a job with yet another BIGGIE - a host whose personality and eyebrows filled the room and most definitely rounded out my career in ways that sizzled more than any of *People* magazine's special year-enders. Stand by, that's coming up next.

Chapter Eleven

BUSHY EYEBROWS (AND THEN SOME)

A herd of political talk shows stampeded into the 1990s with a fiery new brand of hosts from unlikely fields - actors, former governors, boxers, you name it - all pumped up to talk politics. Out of this assembly line of gab in January 1995 came the notably un-political chat show from CBS, one spearheaded and owned by David Letterman called "The Late Late Radio Show with Tom Snyder." Yes, *that* Tom Snyder.

A first of its kind, this live, three-hour entertainment program streamed audio from the television show emanating from LA and wrapped a New York-based radio component around it. Because it was significantly different than anything before, it was also hard to explain when booking the show. The radio portion opened the first 90 minutes and closed the final 30 - and get this, the radio segments weren't always hosted by Tom. In fact, they were rarely hosted by Tom.

Elliott Forest, a former classical music jock (later replaced by Steve Mason, a sports radio guy), filled the nebulous chair. Try explaining THAT to a celebrity or publicist whose client was vying to speak with "Tom and Tom only!"

What follows are some of the offbeat events that popped up on "The Late Late Radio Show with Tom Snyder," thanks to an idiosyncratic host and an unusual format.

How Tom Snyder landed the gig

Tom Snyder and David Letterman had an unusual history. In 1982, after nine years at NBC, Tom Snyder's "The Tomorrow Show" was replaced by an up-and-coming comic. His show was called, "Late Night with David Letterman." For the next six years, Tom hopped from one gig to another - anchoring for WABC-TV "Eyewitness News" in New York, hosting an afternoon talk show on KABC-TV in Los Angeles, and then eventually landing on the ABC Radio Network in 1988, doing a call-in talk show for the next five years. This radio program became a magnet for unexpected celebrity-callers including Ted Koppel of "Nightline" and Sherman Helmsley of "The Jeffersons." Even David Letterman - by that time an established fixture on late-night television - called regularly.

Here's the kicker - when Letterman's show was lured to CBS from NBC in 1993, he was invited to create a new program to follow his at 12:35 am. Guess who he brought over in an unusual pairing of radio and TV? Tom Snyder. He would follow Letterman as he once followed Johnny Carson after "The Tonight Show."

Never underestimate the power of a good joke

The idea that Tom would follow Letterman on television stemmed from a running joke by Letterman himself on his own late-night show, "The Late Show with David Letterman," which in turn escalated into a 1993 episode of "The Larry Sanders Show" (co-created by television/movie genius, Dennis Klein). On that "Life Behind Larry" episode, fictional talk show host Larry Sanders (played by the ground-breaking show's other co-creator, the late Garry Shandling) kidnapped Tom Snyder from Letterman to host a talk show in the slot immediately after his. Tom made a cameo appearance. Television analysts and reviewers raved and later reported that art inspired real life.

Every talk show comes with its own universe of rules

When television and radio producers shared the same host, the "golden rule" applied - the TV producers had more clout and always got first dibs on a guest. Period. Simply, whoever makes the GOLD (that is, bigger bucks for the company) makes the RULES.

However, no one ever said it out loud - until I booked Catherine Bell, who starred as Sarah Mackenzie on the hit new TV series "JAG." She was a producer's "dream guest" because of her colorful talking points. In addition to English, the London-born actress spoke Persian (her mom was born in Iran); she had cancer in her 20s that resulted in the removal of her thyroid (leaving a neck scar that she didn't cover because she thought it was "cool"); she was a huge motorcycle and NASCAR fan; and, though born Catholic, she was studying Scientology. A talk show host like Tom would be the proverbial pig in you-know-what with these topics.

Those of us on the *radio* side of the show had her confirmed for weeks, but guess who was forced to bump their schedule until after *TV* fit the guest into its lineup? Welcome to broadcasting's food chain. From that point on, the radio producers ran guests by the TV producers. We answered to many masters.

When the boss tells a dirty joke, laugh (and with enthusiasm)

Here was another peculiarity of this job. The New York staff never actually met Tom Snyder until four months *after* the show had officially started. Tom and the TV staff were based in Los Angeles, while the radio producers were in New York. For Tom to join us on radio, he'd step out from the TV studio in LA and walk about 300 feet down the hall into a pie sliver of a radio studio where the LA-based engineer rigged him up so we'd all connect.

The New York team - three producers and a producer/ engineer - finally met Tom for the first time after he flew East for meetings with management (and no doubt his "boss" Dave). The 6'4" Tom stepped into our windowless production room crammed with three desks, two printers, a water cooler, and stacks upon stacks of magazines and books. Dressed in a navy sports jacket and an open-collared button-down shirt (which was pretty much his standard uniform on TV), he filled the room, eyebrows and all.

About 30 seconds into this long-awaited first meeting with Tom, the New York team (three guys and a gal) sat completely focused on him as he broke into a smutty joke about a husband, a wife, and a duck (and maybe there was a bar in there, but I don't recall). It got salty. While I like a good dirty joke as much as the next guy, it struck me as the oddest introduction to my new boss. *Why couldn't he have just said hello like other bosses I've had?*

Welcome to the late-night radio Macho Mountain. One thing I learned during my career - if I wanted to keep my gig, I had to get along in the sandbox. And so I'd laugh. Tom was most definitely a cool cat, but in an early-1960s "Mr. Ring-a-Ding-Ding" sort of way. Another throwback to that era, in addition to his stock of dirty jokes, was the pleasure he took in the martini. Well, his version of the adult beverage, something he called a "Snapple-tini."

For one of the biggest radio ad campaigns in the 1990s, Tom spun up his own live copy about Snapple. The company loved it and, as a gesture of appreciation, it sent a year's supply of the beverage. Then Tom reciprocated and invited "Wendy the spokesperson" on-air one night as a guest. She was so much fun, he asked her back.

But here's the shtick. Every Tom fan knew his catch phrase from earlier television days: "Fire up a color-tini, sit back, relax and watch the pictures, now, as they fly through the air." In his 1995 radio version, he'd substitute "Snapple-tini" for "color-tini."

A "Snapple-tini" had a splash of vodka or gin added.

Batman, Birdman - bursting a bubble

We were a SWAT team of four producers who schmoozed with Hollywood-types daily on this celebrity-driven show. We trolled through *TV Guide*, *People* and every hot Hollywood autobiography, then hammered out invitations to A- and B-listers, so we could fill multiple five- to 30-minute segments nightly... only to wake up and do it again the next day. We were ultimate fans on a caffeinated assembly line, freshly assigned to Studio Six - and please God, we did whatever it took to keep the flow going.

One responsibility before bringing guests in studio was to pre-interview them over the phone, asking random questions in hopes of uncovering a unique story or spin. The unexpected "I love my throat scar" detail from Catherine

Bell of "JAG" resulted from one such chatty conversation we shared by phone.

You just never knew what would emerge from these conversations. When I pre-interviewed my favorite childhood crime fighter, Adam West, the actor who played Batman on the late-1960s ABC-TV show, I discovered the man behind the mask was, like his television persona, a campy goofball - as well as a non-stop, talking machine. At the time of this pre-interview in 1995, 30 years had passed since he was chasing bad guys through television's Gotham. (A total of 120 episodes played in reruns for years, inspiring trading cards, action figures, and lunchboxes for fans like me growing up.) Now, Adam West - the actor - was promoting his autobiography, *Back to the Batcave* (Berkley Trade, 1994), which had just come out in paperback.

Within seconds, I recognized that Adam West was freakishly still playing the part. When describing specific television scenes shot with "Catwoman" Julie Newmar, he peppered the phone conversation with action-figure innuendos such as how she "caused curious stirrings in my utility belt." About 15 minutes into our pre-interview, he actually asked for a momentary break so he could go to the "batroom." (Incidentally, the publicist demanded that we stay clear of asking why West was never offered the role of the 1989 "Batman" movie, starring Michael Keaton - which we accommodated. But another host might have ignored the request and even invited Michael Keaton as a follow-up to purposely stir up trouble).

Tom loved the interview because West was so over-the-top campy, especially with this morsel I dug up during the pre-interview: West regularly appeared at public events in full Batman regalia. "Okay, so he's a little nutty," Tom said through the overhead speaker to us back in New York. "But, hey, guys like that keep it fun. And remember, what we do is supposed to be fun."

Tom was a producer's "dream host" because he'd roll with the zaniest of guests.

The mood in the studio always trickles down from the top

The New York Times TV reporter Bill Carter said Tom Snyder captured a unique style that was really more like "performance art" than traditional scripted television. My experience with Tom showed this to be true. He would often talk to the behind-the-scenes staff *while live on air* with the audience watching and listening.

For example, one Friday night in March 1996, the opening theme music for the final portion of the radio show had started and Tom was nowhere to be found. The LA-based engineer was screaming so loudly into his talkback to alert us in New York about the missing host that his voice through the overhead speakers actually rattled the glass in our studio. When Tom was occasionally late for the call on TV, the cameraman panned the empty chair and the announcer joked about it. But on radio? We had no audio equivalent for an empty chair other than dead air. We just kept running the theme music… longer than usual.

Waaaay off mic, thanks to the LA engineer who cranked up the volume as loud as possible, we could hear that familiar laughter (think Dan Aykroyd on "Saturday Night Live" - but MORE SO) grow louder and louder. Finally the scratchy-shuffle sound confirmed that Tom was picking up his headset. The laughter echoed through the airwaves and Tom settled into his chair apologizing, "Sorry folks, my watch is broken and I thought it was a little earlier than it is... and well, let's just do our thing..." Then he laughed his way into the intro of his next guest, comic Drew Carey, who himself was running late and just stepped into the studio after Tom.

Some nights were just off-kilter.

"So tell us about your new book *Dirty Jokes and Beer: Stories of the Unrefined...*" Tom prompted Drew.

As Drew described his bouts with depression while growing up in Cleveland, we could hear, through Tom's mic, a kind of squirming sound as if he were agitated. Finally interrupting Drew, he spoke directly, on-air, to us and asked, "Hey New York, what's with all the hammering?"

We were clueless.

"That hammering - it's way too loud. Is someone trying to break into the building?"

Still, we were stumped. As far as we could determine, the banging sound was isolated in his earpiece. From where, we did not know.

The New York-based engineer frantically checked to see if he had accidentally left the mic open from a remote location. But still, nothing. Now here's where the "performance art" kicked in. At this point, Tom addressed his listeners saying, "Sorry folks I'm hearing a noise that you probably don't hear at home and it's rattling me. Believe me, it's alarming."

Meanwhile, Drew Carey jumped in: "You think the original guest you scheduled tonight has changed his mind and wants back in - trying to break into the studio?"

The noise disappeared - as mysteriously as it began - but the damage was done. Tom was unhinged. We were in for "one of those nights." The fourth-wall was torn down. More trouble ahead.

"Could someone tell me the correct time?" Tom asked on the air. We had no idea where he was going.

The battery-operated clock on the wall in LA that Tom used to time his breaks for commercials was out of sync. Strategically positioned behind the guest, it allowed Tom to surreptitiously glance at the exact time without appearing rude.

Except today. The clock had stopped - four hours earlier. This segment was tanking. No one was paying attention to Drew Carey, who good-naturedly laughed about the whole thing.

"Before we break for a commercial," Tom asked on the air, "would someone please tell me what time it is?"

At which point the engineer opened the mic and groaned the exact time. Drew Carey continued to laugh.

"Well..." Tom asked, "Am I the only one who noticed?"

Phew! The New York staff was relieved it was not our clock.

Tom followed up, "We're taking a break to correct the clock and I correct my attitude."

Upon his return from the commercial, he explained, "Folks... I'm just trying to do an interview here. And some days it's not easy." And then he returned to the regularly scheduled interview, attitude adjusted.

What goes on in the studio usually stays in the studio

On a late-night talk show, there is the risk that a guest will come directly from a boozy dinner party or event half-crocked. Sometimes *totally* crocked. One big-name movie director - who will remain nameless - showed up with an equally inebriated woman with barely a minute to spare before he was scheduled on-air. In the flurry of rushing him behind the mic and on-air, it never occurred to me to give him a breathalyzer. My mistake.

"Hiiiiiii Tooooooom, er, Tommmmm..." he said as soon as we opened his mic.

Making matters worse, the woman attached to this guest's arm in studio was laughing so loudly that she was heard on-air across America through the guest's mic.

"Who is THAT laughing?" the LA-based engineer asked via the "talkback," adding, "Tom's giving me 'the eye'..."

So how did Tom handle the sloshed guest? In an unusual move - he quickly bailed out of the interview. We've had plenty of drunk guests in studio and Tom would usually cruise through. But this guest was more than even Tom could tolerate.

The duo left, we broke for a commercial, and aired out the studio.

Everyone had something to say, at least according to Tom

Johnny Rotten and Jimmy Webb were just two of the many who showed up in-studio soused. What made those interviews fascinating (at least to my producer-ears) was how Tom handled them seamlessly and cool. The guest, on the other hand, didn't always respond in kind. A classic example from Tom's television show currently (as of this writing) on YouTube shows Johnny Rotten growing hostile while Tom tries carrying on a conversation.

While another host might not have invited such an indignant guest back, Tom actually did. Several times. Later he told us why. "I can't think of one instance where I said, 'No, I don't want to do that.' I mean, I didn't want to do Johnny Rotten again, but I did." I'm not quite sure what Tom really meant by that. Perhaps, he enjoyed the personal challenge of dealing with a difficult guest. Or maybe it was part of that whole "performance art" thing and he understood that it held a certain level of fascination for the audience. After all, those YouTube episodes remain quite popular to this day.

Even about TV producer David Milch, a recovering heroin addict and alcoholic, who went on to create both "Deadwood" and "John from Cincinnati," Tom said, "He's a compelling individual... He's nuts, but he's a genius. We do have these people on often, because they've got something to say."

Live guests were not always happy to be there

Another challenge we had with late-hour interviews? Certain guests were agitated about staying up past their bedtime - and they let us know this in their own obnoxious ways. Take Richard Dreyfuss, who was out flacking his flick "Mr. Holland's Opus" and scheduled for 1:30 am.

The interview went something like this:

Tom: You know him from "Jaws" and now, "Mr. Holland's Opus." Welcome our next guest, Richard Dreyfuss.

Dreyfuss: (Complete silence.)

Tom: Welcome, Richard… How are you?

Dreyfuss: (after a pause) Good.

More silence…

For the next excruciating 12 minutes on radio, Dreyfuss proceeded to answer every question Tom tossed at him with one syllable - responses like "Yes," "No," "Yep." Occasionally he threw in a multi-syllabic phrase such as, "Don't know…," "Interesting…," and "Uh-huh." It was brutal. Especially when I was the producer who scheduled the guest. And though it's not fair nor does it really make sense, here's another "Golden Rule" among producers: You Are Only As Good As Your Last Guest.

Tom cut loose the award-winning actor and filled the remaining minutes with his own memories of how beach-going changed during the summer "Jaws" was released. For the next 24 hours, the producers argued whether or not it was a mistake to book Dreyfuss. I took a positive position. Listeners got an unexpected window into someone they thought they knew - and *that's* worth a lot. Although, to this day, I am not totally sure why the normally talkative and friendly actor went mum on Snyder. Again, it might have been the hour.

Expecting the unexpected

"What part of 'no' do you not understand? No dogs upstairs," the CBS receptionist yelled through the phone at me as I eyeballed the studio clock. Eight minutes to go before Joy Behar - and not her two Basset hounds - was scheduled on air.

"But you *must* let her up," I shouted back.

"Don't you tell *me* what to do," the receptionist shrilled back.

"But she's on the air in six minutes..."

"Not with her dogs."

This was getting nowhere fast.

I heard Behar in the background, "If I can't bring them up, I'm leaving,"

"Wait-wait-wait-wait," I shot back. "We're coming downstairs right now," though I had no strategy about getting Behar upstairs.

Think-think-think-think-think....

I was buying time although time was rapidly running out as I came bounding into the lobby.

"Please," I begged the receptionist from hell, "you've got to do this for me and here's why..." still unsure of what I was about to say. Desperation became inspiration and I blurted, "It's my birthday and I can't afford to have one more thing go wrong today." A total fabrication.

She burst out laughing and said, "Are you kidding me? ARE YOU KIDDING WITH ME? It's my birthday today, *too*, and, until this minute, I was feeling sorry for myself. I have company."

Just like that, we bonded. I later brought her an authentic, signed glossy of Tom Snyder. More important, Joy Behar, plus her pups, made it upstairs for the interview. And the listeners got to hear about how she loved her four-legged friends. In fact, she said, she was designing the artwork for doggy t-shirts which she hoped to sell in the future.

Some guests were absolute gems

Walter Cronkite was our official first guest, during the official first hour on the official first night of "The Late Late Radio Show with Tom Snyder." Who better than the man Americans "most trusted" in the news biz to be Tom's welcoming committee at CBS, the network he presided over for 20 years. By this time, the 80-year-old was retired from the business for 14 years and now spending his free time sailing, he told Tom.

Immediately after Tom finished up the over-the-phone interview, I jumped on the line to thank him, never expecting the invitation that followed.

"Take my phone number - and any time you need a guest at the last minute, CALL. I'd talk to Tom any time again." From that night forward, Walter Cronkite was on my short list of people I could call in an emergency. Just for the record, I did just that on the night a guest bailed at the last minute and we brought on Cronkite to discuss the big news of the day. He was the ultimate back-up plan when something went wrong. Sometimes, the bigger the celebrity, the nicer the guy.

Be careful what you say aloud in the studio

With a host 3,000 miles away and a show that started long after sundown, the posture of the New York staff was casual. The halls were semi-dark and dead, even the cleaning people were gone for the day. Over the summer, we commonly wore shorts and T-shirts to work. Sometimes, however, the loose environment created loose lips.

I recall an embarrassing moment with celebrated concert performer Bob McGrath, best known as "Bob" from "Sesame Street." McGrath was out doing the circuit on radio and TV, promoting his latest book, *Uh Oh! Gotta Go! Potty Tales from Toddlers* (Barron's Educational Series, 1996).

Unaware that McGrath was being escorted at that very moment into the studio behind me, I hit the talkback to ask the engineer a pretty insensitive question, "Bob McGrath is still alive?"

"Not only that," came the voice from behind me, "he's still walking as well."

McGrath, being a gracious man, laughed as he reached out his hand to shake mine. I was mortified… but learned a valuable lesson.

Always be ready with Plan B

Hot guests are known to cancel at the last minute so experienced producers are always ready with a backup. You just never knew where that next guest was hiding.

For example, I found a gem 3,000 miles away while trying to send show materials from New York to the studio in LA on its broken fax machine. I phoned it to the attention of the West Coast late-night IT guy and discovered that this nice techie named Johnny Whittaker was, in fact, the childhood actor who played "Jody" on the late-1960s/early-1970s CBS-TV sitcom "Family Affair."

So one night when a celebrity dropped out at the last minute, Tom interviewed the actor-turned-IT-guy about his story bouncing in and around Hollywood.

When last-minute opportunities like that didn't appear, what was a producer to do? We booked Tom Snyder himself. He was excellent at the improvisational monologue. On one such occasion, the audience learned that Tom loved Lionel Trains and owned a set that ran through two rooms in his California home. Years after "The Late Late Radio Show" went dark, Tom narrated and appeared on two different videos - one called "A Century of Legendary Lionel Trains," which celebrated 100 years of Lionel Trains, and the other called "Celebrity Train Layouts 2: Tom Snyder," featuring his own collection.

Grace under fire – while being fired!

After just four-and-a-half years, "The Late Late Radio Show with Tom Snyder" went dark in March 1999. CBS management called to inform us that Tom was retiring from both radio and TV and therefore so were we.

We were numb.

Years later, I watched Tom's final television show on YouTube and noticed that he took it in stride, completely matter-of-factly. Could it be that he had been through this so many times before? What struck me by his gracious manner was only seconds before his final show, a promo ran for Tom's replacement, Craig Kilborn. Tom's goodbye hour was without a hint of self-pity or bitterness.

In fact, he thanked everyone by name for "the 887 nights" we all worked together. Then, to the audience, he said, "You who have watched me and listened to me on radio and on television for over 25 years in this country... you're great people to work for in this time period... because you get it and because you understand it and because your curiosity and interest in things surpass those who listen in other day-parts - I am convinced of that." He even wore a tie that night.

We subsequently heard that he moved to the San Francisco Bay Area with his "companion" - his word for the woman in his life - to be near his daughter and grandchildren.

There's hope after retirement

Sometime in 2005, about seven years after his "retirement," Tom announced on his website that he had chronic lymphocytic leukemia. He wrote that "as a child, if you heard that someone had 'leukemia,' it was considered a death sentence. Now my doctors say it's treatable!"

Tom Snyder died on July 29, 2007 at the age of 71. He donated his Lionel train set to the New Jersey Hirailers, where it remains on display.

He deserves to be remembered as one of the most original and unique talents to grace the modern era of talk media.

Chapter Twelve

TOOK A LEAP

For the first time in nearly 20 years of working as a talk show producer, I was actually shaken up by the sudden cancellation of my Tom Snyder gig. Perhaps, this was simply the result of me getting older, or maybe just going around the track one too many times. I had lost not only a slick job, but also, my daily mojo. Gone was that buzz that woke me before the alarm and launched me into my day. If my life were a talk show, I'd now be dead air.

Instead of rolling over and playing dead, I took this as a sign to recharge my batteries and overhaul my life. I packed up a suitcase, traded in my New York subway tokens and headed west to Marina del Rey, California, a boating community just south of Los Angeles. At the very least, it was sunny there.

Reinventing myself

I wasn't the only one to hatch such a makeover in life. Some of the more colorful talk show hosts I had met or worked with over the years had taken far greater leaps after *their* job losses… from which I found inspiration.

By the time Glenn Beck was 30, he had hopscotched from one radio gig to another, from Seattle, to Baltimore, then Houston, Phoenix, and New Haven. As he explained to *The Wall Street Journal* years after this low point, "Nobody would work with me. I was friendless, hopeless, [and] suicidal. I had lost my family. I bottomed out, [and] didn't know what to do. I actually thought I was going to be a chef - go to work in a kitchen someplace."

By June 2013, however, thanks to a life overhaul, Beck's net worth - according to *Forbes* Celebrity 100 - was $90 million. Part of that came from the launch of his pioneering online media platform, The Blaze.

Rush Limbaugh experienced a transition as well. In 1974, after a series of top 40 DJ jobs, Rush yet again found himself unemployed. As he walked out the door on his last day at KQV, Pittsburgh, the manager who fired him strongly suggested that he switch from the "talent" side of the business to sales. Instead, Limbaugh traded in any radio aspirations that still simmered inside for a $12,000-a-year position as director of promotions with the Kansas City Royals major league baseball team. For the next five years, he was haunted by the career he loved. So, in 1984, when a small-town opportunity came up, he turned down a big salary job with a potato chip distribution business and instead took another shot behind the microphone. This time he got traction, eventually working his way up the chain of markets and landing in Sacramento, the frenzied conservative capital of California, to replace, of all people, loudmouthed, nicotine-addicted, Morton Downey Jr. on KFBK. The rest is history.

Let's not leave out Larry King. Long before there was an Oprah Winfrey, Larry King was a Miami multimedia star in the 1970s working in radio, TV, and newspapers. He played records at WIOD-AM, hosted WTVJ-TV's "Miami Undercover," and wrote a gossip column for the *Miami Herald*. Then, on December 20, 1971, he simultaneously lost all three Miami gigs after being charged with grand larceny (in a convoluted case tied to money involved in the JFK assassination investigation). At the time, he was in mega-debt.

As Larry explains in *My Remarkable Journey* (Weinstein Books, 2009), "Pretty soon I wouldn't even be able to afford cigarettes." With just 10 dollars left in his pocket, or so the "story" goes, he made a lucky two-dollar bet at the racetrack and collected $8,000 - enough to make a fresh start in Louisiana as a publicist for a racetrack.

Though hardly sitting on the throne of success like these broadcasters, I chose to channel their wisdom. I, too, could soldier on and try something new. It's not like "a big eraser in the sky" (to borrow from author Anne Lamott) would descend upon me and eliminate my entire work history. I was armed with 20 years of hard-earned experience. While my most recent job went kaput, my talents were alive and well on my resume: "attention to details; ability to meet deadlines; respect for a time-bullied industry." I had marketable experience.

With sand lodged between my toes, I cast my hook out to an ocean of TV and film gigs, purposely aiming for ones I'd never dreamed of landing. It was time to reinvent myself.

Screenus envy

But first, a certain truth that most radio people are hesitant to admit (though it's key to our psyche): Everyone who's been anyone in radio - engineer, host, producer, mail clerk - at one time or another has wanted OUT. If any one of them ever denies it, don't believe them. They are big fat liars - very likely lying to themselves as well as you. Radio people have always suffered from inferiority complexes likely due, in part, to our lower salaries compared to our counterparts in television. I've worked in both fields and can confidently report this to be true.

Plus, TV has a much bigger, although, intangible buzz than radio. There is the feeling among many that being on TV makes one "realer" than just being real.

Radio and TV cover the same events - including political conventions, primaries, and national disasters - so producers in both camps will compete for the same guests. We all jump through equal hoops, whether in trying to land a senator, an actor, or the founder of Microsoft. Radio and TV producers alike must schmooze the handler, set up a car service for transport to and from the studio, stock the green room fridge with organic grapes (or whatever the guest requests), write up the talking points for the host, and blah-blah-blah-blah-blah. The work was the same, the payoff not. Guests, being guests, know the perceived power of television, and needless to say, will bump radio for a chance to appear on the tube. That's 100 out of 100 times. Radio producers have learned to reschedule knowing such is the food chain of the entertainment industry and radio's lot in the world. Irritating? Yes!

What eats away at a radio producer's psyche? We earn smaller salaries, stay in cheaper hotels on the road, and overall must make do with less. I saw this up close in February 2000 while covering the New Hampshire primaries for ABC News Radio. As radio reporters and producers shuttled around to our respective interviews in one shared car, TV people - with their bigger budgets - were each driving their own cars around town.

If you can't beat 'em, join 'em

Now, reinventing myself in LA, I aimed for the bigger paycheck and targeted every TV and film company that I could (and yes, to be safe, I did shoot out a few resumes to Los Angeles-based radio stations). I landed a job in television, as a field researcher for "Judge Mills Lane," the courtroom show hosted by the charismatic former boxing referee.

My mission was to prowl through stacks of small claims files at Los Angeles courthouses and track down guests willing to have their cases heard on national television. I was but one of a brigade of "researchers" from competing shows like "Judge Judy" and "The People's Court."

In Beverly Hills, Hollywood, Malibu, Culver City, and Santa Monica, I'd pore through hundreds of testimonies written by unfortunate souls spilling out their hearts, crying for help. They were victims of disastrous dates set up by fly-by-night matchmaking services, a roommate's stinky closet, dog bites, patched roofs that still leaked, failed attempts to remove facial hair by laser treatment, fake engagement rings, sloppy paint jobs, loud neighbors, careless dry cleaners, broken noses... you name it.

Who knew at the time I accepted this job that I'd gain a rich insider's peek behind the judicial curtain? It wasn't so much a courthouse that I entered but a real life "Twilight Zone" - and the strangest cross-section of humankind and activities ever assembled under one roof.

And it was all public record. (That's right. You, too, can travel to your local courthouse today and have yourself a voyeuristic hoot.)

I rifled through miles and miles of pending cases that were on the docket. During a busy week, as many as 500 cases were filed in the Beverly Hills location alone. During a slow week, such as holiday times like Thanksgiving, Yom Kippur or Christmas - maybe only 150.

Each case that I nabbed which made it on the air landed money in my pocket. Sometimes it really added up. Believe me, I wasn't the only one celebrating. Individuals who agreed to argue their cases on national television landed a "free" trip to New York City, where the show was taped, and an overnight stay at the Marriott in Times Square. If the plaintiff won the case and the defendant had to pay up, the TV show picked up the costs of the claim.

Reality television

What made for a great case for television? One that was loaded with disputes, human drama and emotions - which were heightened when the suit was between family members, ex-lovers or neighbors. As a field researcher, I'd decrypt the sentence or two written by the plaintiff on the claims form. It was the job of the show's producers to call the subjects and gauge if they were a) articulate, b) sufficiently "worked up," and c) interested and available to physically come onto the TV show. Overall, the more horrendous the story, the better, though a quirky, over-the-top delivery by someone could trump anything and everything.

Admittedly - some of the cases I dug up in Hollywood (or "Holly-weird," as my executive producer back in New York called it), were, let's just say, *zany*. In fact, at one point, she questioned the status of these plaintiffs asking, "Are these people real, or are they *actors*?"

"Janel," I told her, "This is Hollywood. Here, *everyone's* an actor."

What follows is a sampling of the tortured souls she questioned:

"I suffered overwhelming trauma during a pedicure when I placed my feet into a bacteria-infested foot basin. The owner is obviously violating the health code."

"I wore a shoulder-eating bra with a strap that dug through to the bone."

"She trespassed on my property, stole the garage door opener, and cut the Club off the steering wheel of my car."

"My cheapskate brother refuses to share expenses for our mother's casket."

"My ex-boyfriend has caused me undue hardship, having sued me for $233. Now I want to counter his act and make sure that he is not going to sue me for flowers, dinners, and Christmas gifts he gave me willingly."

"My claim for $2000 results from two damaged lamps, a slashed oriental rug, and a ripped sweater." He added, "The defendant proceeded to break my living room window and kicked a hole in the front door." Details in the paperwork revealed that they shared the same address.

"I loaned my girlfriend a credit card, only to discover she bought a new wardrobe as well as dinner for her new boyfriend."

Court rat

As the weeks on this job unfolded, I became an extended member of the family-like staff at the various courthouses. I'd huddle over the metal cabinets and sort through the files, as people from all walks of life lined up within earshot, talking to - sometimes yelling at - the county court clerks standing before them whose jobs were to guide them through the paperwork. These women - and they all were women - would calmly answer questions while tempers flared and tears shed before them. The litigants, obviously angered enough to drag themselves to the courthouse to file paperwork, sometimes came to near-blows with the clerks, in what was obviously misdirected anger and frustration over their claims.

At times, I'd have to fight the impulse to yell back at some of the nastiest visitors. It took my all. More mind-boggling than anything was that I never witnessed a clerk lose her cool. Not once.

Kay was a great Zen-like example of this and someone I befriended while at the Beverly Hills courthouse. For the half-dozen years our paths crossed, this Sherri Shepherd lookalike credited the gospel music that quietly streamed from her desk radio for soothing her soul. That, she said, was her antidote to it all.

I knew she was full of heart the first week we met, when a man entered the courthouse weeping over his wife who just left him - though, as he told us, this was *not* the reason he was there. In fact, he said he was registering a complaint about a neighbor who ran out of town after borrowing a few thousand dollars to pay his rent. When Kay heard the whole story, she sprang up from her desk behind the counter and gave him a hug.

Another guy who dropped by also got a lot of attention - but that's because he was movie-star handsome. In fact, even "Trish-the-Lip" (who owned every shade of lipstick and had a great work ethic) stopped herself from filing, stood up straighter, smoothed her jacket, and smiled directly at him. Oddly enough, he kept signaling to people standing behind him to cut ahead until finally the crowd dispersed and he was standing solo at the counter. He leaned in and whispered his questions to Kay, inspiring all kinds of curiosity from the rest of us. When he finally left, his paperwork filled out, I scanned his file, figuring this had to be good. Sure enough, he was suing "The Lonely Hearts Malibu Matchmaker" for "horrible dates with horrible women." *He* went to a matchmaker? We were stunned.

Surprise was always another breath away. Just when I thought I'd heard it all, along came cases that were so off-the-charts wacko that even the courthouse had a file cabinet for disputes that were dismissed. They included the woman who claimed she cracked her front tooth on a Wise potato chip; the man suing the supermarket for bones found in his boneless steak; and the tattoo magazine model taking her tattoo artist to task for "poorly executed work." (Given that her entire body was covered in ink, you couldn't tell *where* the mistake was made.)

Some days, I left the courthouse with my eyeballs spinning. But not Kay. As a 30-year veteran clerk, she observed, "Thank goodness for a stronger economy. People don't seem to be as lawsuit-crazy as they were a decade ago." She added, "Back then, it was a real zoo."

For about six years, I juggled my courthouse gig, as well as a few freelance ones that came along, (like hacking out articles for women's magazines and teaching writing classes at Loyola Marymount). All the while, I was living a third-class existence paying first-class rent on an old 1966 houseboat moored along a dock in the largest manmade marina in the United States. But, I was quite happy with this new existence. Since "escaping" New York, I felt that I was living the dream... at least *my* dream... at the time.

Having found a new joy of life, I thought I'd never return to the Big Apple.

And then, along came September 11, 2001 and with it, a new reality.

Chapter Thirteen

ANOTHER DAY, ANOTHER TERROR

On the morning of September 11, 2001, in the pre-attack hours, a handful of disparate headlines dominated the news and talk show circuit around the country...

Colin Powell: "Why his star somehow shines less brightly than expected" (*Time*)

Bush's Fuzzy Science: "The President's calculation of what makes 'viable stem-cell lines'" (*Time*)

Andrea Yates: "Competency hearing begins Tuesday" (CNN)

JonBenet Ramsey Case: "Colorado police look into possible lead on AOL" (CNN)

Gary Condit Case: "U.S. Rep. Gary Condit still not a suspect... ethical questions on heels of his admitted extramarital affair with intern Chandra Levy" (*The New York Times*)

Radio Morning Show Stuff: "Howard Stern puts a feel on Loni Anderson during dinner" ("The Howard Stern Show")

That last topic dominated late-morning on the self-dubbed "King of All Media" program – Howard Stern's New York City-originated/nationally syndicated show that was at the peak of its terrestrial radio dominance. Howard had dinner with Loni the night before and specifically, his words were, "We were screwing around, you know, just kissing...

nothing heavy." All of which became fodder for talk during the drive-time portion of the following morning's program. Until 8:57 am, that is.

Journalism Sternalism

At that moment, Howard broke the momentum of conversation among his somewhat lascivious sidekicks (Gary Dell'Abate, Robin Quivers, and others) to say, "I don't mean to interrupt the fun, but this is a breaking news story... a *serious* news story. A plane has crashed into the World Trade Center." The following is an abbreviated version of a round-table of responses.

"You're kidding?" Robin exclaimed.

"The World Trade Center is on fire," Howard calmly reported.

"What is going on?" Robin interjected.

"Really? Let me look out my window," said Rob, a regular who joined the crew by phone from his downtown apartment, physically within view of the towers.

"See it?" Howard asked. "Take a look, seriously."

"I don't see any fire," Rob responded.

"That's the Financial Building," someone said with disbelief followed by other chatter.

Seconds later, Rob returned, an obvious change in his voice, "Dude! DUDE! Oh My God... The whole thing is on fire... I mean, not a little fire... It's huge."

Cut off from the real world in a windowless, isolated studio, no one could imagine how truly serious this was - a terrorist attack and not "simply" a plane crash. Without any new developments reported on the news, the conversation, thus, swung back to Loni's body parts.

Until Howard interrupted again, this time streaming live audio to the listening audience from CBS-TV while his team analyzed the visuals they viewed in studio, this was Mystery Science Theater 3000, Howard-style. Here are some soundbites:

"Looks like a movie," Robin said, commenting on the scene's surrealism.

"There's a piece of the plane hanging off the side of the building."

"Huge fire."

"It's like 'The Towering Inferno'... Like once it gets started, what happens?"

"Imagine being trapped in there."

"How are they going to get hoses up there? They are going to have to rely on the sprinkler system."

"And you know how well they work in the city..."

"You can't drag a hose up there?"

"Don't they have a ladder that goes that high?"

"I don't even know how you begin to fight that fire..."

"This is going to be massive... Emergency crews are rushing to the scenes."

Intuitive spontaneity

Producer Gary Dell'Abate - one of Howard's closed circle of high-echelon sidekicks - then said something listeners would never hear on news stations anywhere else on radio, "It's a terrorist attack, isn't it?"

By the time the second tower was hit 18 minutes later, the Stern crew connected dots and moved the story forward - nearly 100 percent correctly. News reporters up and down the dial were straight-jacketed, mostly repeating and repeating only that which they knew could be verified. In the case of Stern, it was a rare example of unrestrained speculation during a breaking story actually being ahead of the pack AND correct.

When one of Howard's cohorts asked, "Why doesn't the news just call it like it is?" Gary the producer piped up again, "They're a legit news organization - they're not allowed to say what we're thinking."

And in that simple truth, he honed in on talk radio's purpose: a place where people can discuss the messy, prejudiced, and sometimes ugly parts of life, speaking from a less-tailored part of the brain. Radio people are notorious for poor spelling and unkempt hair and wardrobe. Even callers know they can anonymously say the sorts of stuff normally shared with a friend over the bathroom stall.

On the morning of 9/11, thousands of commuters heading into New York City were frozen in traffic on bridges, tunnels, and highways with no clue what was unfolding beyond the bumper of the car in front of them. Except those tethered to

Howard who were ear-witnessing an unfamiliar seriousness seldom heard on this usually raucous show. It was all part of the "new normal" Americans were about to enter. Howard and his band of bawdy street rogues stamped real language on the horror, even targeted suspects. By 9:20 that morning, they turned out to be pretty accurate - it *was* a terrorist attack. They just didn't deliver it with polished elocution or perfectly parted hair.

A fertile new environment for talk radio intensity

The events of September 11 reminded me why I first became a talk show producer - and more important as I worked in television some 3,000 miles away in Los Angeles, why I craved returning to the trenches of New York City and my old line of work. In a mind-boggling disaster such as this, a producer is on the front lines, not only trying to find answers to the *why* something happened, but the *who* to explain it.

Upheaval was everywhere, not just stirring inside me. A strange new level of cooperation, though temporary, emerged - competitors up and down the dial pooled resources, music-only formats switched to talky, less-tuney ones. Even wall-to-wall news stations broke format and took phone calls from listeners. Radio resorted to what it does best - tapping into the unlimited possibilities of the spoken word, delivering a deeper understanding of the feelings and fears that emerge in all of us. Instead of isolation and confusion, there was community. Callers on the "front line," working or living in view of the towers, were shuffled to the front of the deck to speak to the host. Chilling stories of lost loved ones were emerging for days afterwards.

During disasters such as this, a true broadcaster will find the gumption to do whatever it takes - pull 16-hour-shifts while colleagues fan out into the community for man-on-the-street reports and nap on an office couch. Take a shower? Eat breakfast? There's always time for that later.

Back to where I once belonged

Within eight weeks, I answered my own "call to duty" and returned to New York City. I found my "mojo" on the West Coast but as it turned out, it brought me back to where I started. I found my inner compass.

Years earlier, a former news director said it best during his own call to duty after driving back to work from New Jersey in a blackout to lend a hand to those of us working the lobster shift. "You don't always choose a career. Sometimes a career chooses you."

But first, I had to land a job. After the towers fell, so did the economy. Major companies were packing up and leaving. Job interviews were tough to land.

Salem Communications syndicated talk host Mike Gallagher (one of the nicest hosts in the business, as well as one of the most successful) needed a backup producer at his studio on the 18th floor of the Empire State Building (of all places). In this post-Twin Towers era, the 1,250-foot landmark was again the tallest building (and target) in the Big Apple.

What was once a 15-minute commute now took more than double that time. The subway was a nightmare. Military personnel - armed with Uzis, AK-47s, and gasmasks hanging from their belts - randomly stopped commuters below the entrance to search backpacks. We were now in the era of

"If you see something, say something." From the moment I left my home, I was both scanning and being scanned.

The city streets were foreboding. I was just one block away from my interview at the Empire State Building, when a garbage pail on the sidewalk barreled over and boomed - make that BOOMED. Anyone within feet of it, leaped. Innocently enough, a driver pulling into a temporary parking spot accidentally hit the barrel. Talk about the jitters!

Before heading to the 18th floor, I had to pass through a human barrier of military personnel while backpacks, briefcases, purses and other "carry-ons" went through scanners on conveyor belts. Once upstairs, Mike Gallagher's regular producer/engineer Eric Hansen greeted me with the words, "Welcome to the 'other target,'" a nickname the guys gave to the historic building.

Amidst this nightmarish version of New York in transition, I trained with Eric as he planned multiple days off. Later, I came to learn the reason. He and Gallagher were house-hunting in Texas, where they planned to relocate their families and the show - and with it, a portion of my freelance work. Like a number of other companies, they left New York City for a feeling of greater security.

I had to drum up more work.

Mid-game adjustment

Freelancing was a career path all its own. Especially my willingness to work the toughest shifts to fill - weekends, vacation relief, morning drive (4:00 am through 12:00 noon), even the dreaded overnights. It was what I needed to do to get work and re-enter the business in New York. For program directors and managing editors who needed to fill oddball shifts, I became a welcome "solution" - a highly competent convenience. I never said no. As a result, I was repeatedly asked to return to my old stomping grounds at CBS, ABC, and local WOR - as well as several others.

If there was one thing these various news organizations shared, it was the lingo of this post-9/11 era. Think "color-codes."

Welcome to the real brave new world

About six months after the attack in New York, the Department of Homeland Security introduced a five-color-coded system that purported to identify the "risk" of a terror attack throughout a given day: green (low), blue (guarded), yellow (elevated), orange (high), and red (severe). News organizations not only weaved the color into the news each day, but also included it on their websites, updating the alerts with embedded widgets from the Department of Homeland Security. It was like the Weather Channel's obsession with various levels of symbols and designations ("watches," "alerts," "warnings," etc.) during a hurricane.

As a roving freelance producer, I followed this new color-lingo religiously. During the next four-plus years that codes were used, the threat level hit orange (high) five times, including the days surrounding the first anniversary of September 11th and days affiliated with a Muslim religious holiday.

Only once did the threat level rise to red. That was August 10, 2006 (and it stayed there through the fifth anniversary of 9/11), when British authorities identified a major plot threatening commercial flights from the United Kingdom to the United States.

Looking back now, the lingo was problematic. As Rep. Bennie Thompson, (D-Mississippi) stated, "The color-coded system taught Americans to be scared, not prepared. Each and every time the threat level was raised, very rarely did the public know the reason, how to proceed, or for how long to be on alert." I hate to think that we in the media were contributing to an atmosphere of fear but hindsight is 20/20.

The fear of future attacks prompted a new programming focus: *security.* Producers scurried for freshly emerging experts - some, reporters who had been following al Qaeda all along, such as Peter Bergen, a regular CNN contributor. Special terrorism news beats emerged with correspondents popping up at the Pentagon, the White House, and Homeland Security desks at various hotspots around the world. Amazingly, the nationally-syndicated version of the Sean Hannity radio show debuted on September 10 - the very day before 9/11! Of course, it went on to become one of the most important news/talk radio shows of the modern era. Talk about the moon and the stars lining up... News/talk radio became a conversation center for the new reality.

American provincialism

Many American experts we booked were limited by a glaring blind spot - a provincial perspective of the world. As a producer, I began searching for intelligence experts with a broader scope. One such individual was former Israeli counter-terrorism intelligence officer Juval Aviv.

Once affiliated with the Mossad, he reported to Congress that the United States was hardly prepared for the threats that were brewing. When it came to terrorism, we Americans were amateurs and he wasn't shy to specify this on the air.

Shortly after 9/11, Aviv conducted a series of tests in five major American cities. In broad daylight, he placed an empty briefcase in public spaces - a street corner, next to a garbage can, and on a park bench. Then, he waited. His goal? To learn if Americans were tuned into potential dangers. Not one person contacted the police to report the abandoned bag. "In Chicago," Aviv added, "someone tried to steal it!"

He described potential attacks of the future - in shopping malls, rush hour subways, busy train stations. Furthermore, he predicted they would happen right before our eyes - in Disneyland, Las Vegas casinos, any number of Manhattan landmarks - as well as in rural America such as Wisconsin and North Dakota. "The American government knows all this, but just doesn't want to terrify the public with the facts," he would say. As of the time of this writing, whether or not he was correct, we might not know for another hundred years.

Overexposure to fear

The cumulative effect of working as a freelance news producer during these days and hearing stories like this, day in and day out, took its toll. When terrorism was all you talked about, terrorism became all you thought about. I was a walking-talking, color-coded-thinking producer. If I saw something, I said something. I was becoming increasingly edgy and hyper.

Consider Wallid Shoebat - a kind of wannabe "talking head," whose publicist contacted me about three times in 2002 and who was not yet seen on television or heard on radio. It's so much easier to follow the herd of producers and book a guest who popped up the day before on Sean Hannity, Anderson Cooper, or NPR. By the third time I heard about this "one-time radicalized Muslim willing to die for the cause of Jihad," that is, until he converted to Christianity in 1994, I thought to myself I had nothing to lose.

Wallid was mysterious. He had no book (translation: no food chain of editors who verified his story). He had no history as a guest on talk shows (not Larry King, Chris Matthews, or *any*one, for that matter). He had no contact info - other than a few blogs on the internet. And he wasn't willing to come to the studio.

"He can only be a 'phoner,'" his publicist stated, because he was fearful of exposing himself to the anti-Muslim culture. Furthermore, get this - the publicist refused to give me Wallid's direct phone number to call. Instead, he said, Wallid would call me in the studio with a blocked line, to secure the secrecy of his phone number. Basically, he and Wallid broke every rule I had regarding a guest. What was a producer to do?

I booked him anyway.

If he were telling the truth, he had an amazing story. And besides, *what's the worst that could happen?*

I warned the hosts about this guest's sketchiness - he might not be who and what he said he was, but if I were willing to take a chance, perhaps so should they. Clearly, this added to the "fun" of breaking ground in booking a guest and some of the hosts were eating it up.

On the day of the interview, all logistics fell into place - the biggest of all, Wallid. He reconfirmed the interview early that morning, exactly the time he promised. Then he called in later that morning at the designated time to join us on air. He began to tell a riveting story.

"I was a radicalized Muslim willing to die for the cause of Jihad... My mother was an American and my father, a Palestinian Arab. As a member of the PLO, I was involved in terror activity, and, at one point, imprisoned in Jerusalem for three weeks. It was in prison where I was recruited to plant a bomb in Bethlehem as a result of which, thank God, no one was injured."

I was frozen to every word, as were the hosts interviewing him. And then something happened that had never occurred before on any one of my shows. Wallid broke into a foreign Middle Eastern language.

I shut off his mic right in the middle of whatever he was saying. I stopped breathing and my heart went into overdrive. Like in a Hollywood movie, time slowed down, the voices got louder, and a "Code Red" alarm sounded in my ears... The host conducting the interview was stumped, asking, "Wallid? Wallid, are you there?" And then he repeated it, asking louder and louder.

I ignored the host, and instead yelled through the talkback, "Wallid! WALLID!! You cannot do that."

"What? What? Cannot do *what*???"

"You cannot talk in another language!"

"What do you mean? Why?"

"English! Speak English. This is an English-speaking radio show... You don't speak another language here. You speak English." Fortunately, he responded positively to my urgent command and resumed speaking English.

Call me insane, but in my adrenaline-crazed, hyper-vigilant producer mind, I imagined this guest unleashing an army of sleeper cells around the country. My reasoning in the snap of the moment - if multiple terrorists armed with box cutters can highjack four airplanes and fly passengers, including themselves, to their deaths, why couldn't something just as absurd as what I imagined happen? I know, I was drowning in the drama.

When you sat where I did on the other side of the glass, hour after hour, day after day, and heard warning after warning, you couldn't help but develop a new filter on the world. Maybe a little tilted, maybe loaded with my own self-made triggers. I had now witnessed it for months on the streets of New York City with the roar of an airplane overhead, the backfire of a car, or the bumbling tumble of a garbage pail. I was a jumpy New Yorker - just more so.

Wallid took a deep breath. I took a bigger one. He promised to finish the interview in English. And he did.

Over the days and weeks that followed, I subsequently saw him on Fox News Channel's "Hannity & Colmes," CNN's "Anderson Cooper 360," as well as other cable news shows. Along the way, he left a trail of equally skeptical producers. We emailed each other asking opinions about his credibility. We blogged on our company websites. We talked about him at radio conventions, or when we bumped into one another on the street. Soon enough the subject dropped. No one, it seemed, ever truly got a clear hold on his back-story. Or was the heart of his mystery that he was just so culturally foreign?

Producers were paid to produce. Frankly, we were off-and-running with the next segment even before having completed the one unfolding in "real time." We were producers, as our job title suggested. Find-confirm-produce... move a new segment forward each day until the next breaking story and expert with buzz could slice-and-dice the raw materials at hand. We were only as good as our last guest - usually a fear-driving, agent of gloom-and-doom in the post-9/11 era.

After 18 months of cobbling together freelance gigs around the clock, I landed full-time at United Stations Radio Networks, corralling both celebrity and news-talk guests in a high-pressure job called a satellite tour producer. Up, up and away...

Chapter Fourteen

WHERE'S THE SATELLITE?

Here's a secret. What listeners may believe is a live, in-studio interview at their local station is sometimes, in reality, unfolding between microphones thousands of miles apart from each other.

The local host is connected by various kinds of digital techno-magic to a guest who sits afar in a studio in some other city - a guest whose handlers hope to cram him or her into as many assembly-line interviews as possible. How that guest is positioned onto multiple stations, escorted by car to and from a central location, fed, seated, mic-checked, and prepped, is often thanks to what's called a "satellite tour" producer.

In the 1990s, transmissions between remote guests and hosts were actually relayed by satellite. However, extreme high-fidelity digital telephone lines (largely) replaced satellites. The most popular such telephone line is still in use: ISDN or Integrated Systems Digital Network. A newer form of internet connectivity - VoIP (Voiceover Internet Protocol) - has become more popular.

Despite this transition, the name "satellite tour" remained in the lingo to describe the process. So, during this phase of my career, I was constantly being asked, "Where's the satellite?" Sort of like, where's the egg in an egg cream?

This new breed of booker became a shadow member of multiple staffs around the country, providing extra guest interviews and prep work for those daily productions. He or she was usually employed at network companies like ABC, CBS, FOX, Premiere, or United Stations Radio Networks (USRN) and super-served the affiliated hosts by sending bios, books, video clips - whatever it took to prepare the segment. In return, the local station might run an inventory of network commercials, as in good old-fashioned barter, or set up some other business-to-business arrangement such as paying cash.

A lone wolf who's often obsessed with pop culture and news, the satellite producer hounded for guests by dogging the publicity departments at television networks, movie studios, publishing houses, magazines, and the handlers for Capitol Hill and other politicos, hoping to sniff out just about any household name-of-the-week. The guest's publicist in turn got to hype his or her client on multiple outlets, then unfurled the list of stations covered in a short amount of time back to the boss.

Ideally, that guest was live in studio. But if necessary, they connected by phone. (What – I would say no to George Clooney if he was only available by phone?)

Assembly line producer

From 2001 through 2008, I worked as a satellite producer for over 120 news/talk stations via my job at USRN. Rarely, if ever, did any host ever acknowledge on-air that I existed. What host wanted to admit he or she was part of a parade of gabbers, hyping a guest who in 10 minutes would be yapping up similar chat in Miami, Nashville, or Chicago? To help foster that unique and personal gab and help the guest on a tour keep the interview fresh, I'd coach each to enthusiastically greet the hosts by name and act as if they went out for drinks the previous night.

The aim was to sound very warm and fuzzy. It was a schmooze-fest and my job was to help the guest ease through any conversational barriers.

In the course of an hour, I'd set up as many as 10 interviews, each lasting five to 10 minutes. When the system was working, each host hit the 10-minute allotted time, allowing me to reposition the guest seamlessly onto the next station with hardly a breath in between. It was like double-dutch jump rope while wearing earphones and punching up the right buttons on the console in front of me.

Anything could - and did - happen once I popped open the mic. Join me in this next chapter for a few unexpected moments and an assortment of freaky guests...

Chapter Fifteen

TALK SHOW, FREAK SHOW

A compelling talk show guest a) told a good story, b) taught something new, and c) made you laugh. That was on a good day.

Once the producers popped open a live mic, anything could happen. Or, as the very first producer who trained me once warned, "Expect the unexpected." This was talk radio, after all. A guest dropped the F-bomb (though most knew they shouldn't), arrived straight from a boozy dinner party buzzed, and/or just had a raging argument with his or her spouse. How easy a segment could derail as indicated in earlier chapters of this book.

Jekyll & Hyde

Over time, I noticed that many guests fell into certain offbeat categories. Nearly every celebrity I met in a casual studio setting presented a different persona than the one they showed on television or in the media. It was jarring when that face was so *dramatically* different. Join me from my front-row seat for a handful of those surprising experiences:

David Letterman

The man who surpassed Johnny Carson for having the longest late-night hosting career on American television ranks in my roster as the most introverted of all guests and, well, so unlike his smooth persona on CBS. David Letterman is the only guest I've ever "met," whom I never *technically, literally* met. Yet, for one solid hour, I sat a mere eight inches away.

Letterman and his four-person entourage stopped in the hallway just outside the control room, when one of the women spotted me testing out the equipment and, without so much as "Hello..." she asked, "Where's the studio?"

Before I could compute who she was among the pack (or the man behind her, his face overshadowed by a drawn baseball cap), I pointed through the glassed-in studio. A moment later, the studio door swung open and that man plunked himself down in a chair opposite a mic, the baseball cap still drawn. You'd never know this was the same guy who parachuted into millions of viewers' bedrooms nightly. A few seconds later, he shifted the chair so his back faced me in the control room, where he remained cemented for the next hour to handle a series of interviews.

For the entire segment, the back of David Letterman's head, his neck, and his navy sweatshirt were inches away from my grasp - well, realistically, if my super-powers allowed me to glide through the glass that separated us. If *Page Six* was looking for a piece of gossip, the only juice I could offer was the tag's message peeking out from his collar, "Champion, Size L." It was downright bizarre to be in such close proximity to someone for an hour and not be acknowledged on any level.

Dave's handlers, the four who paraded in with him that night, had now stepped into the control room and bickered over whether Dave wanted red or green apples. (They settled on green.) They next bickered over who would actually go out and buy these apples and settled on the youngest, an intern, no doubt. Was Dave that persnickety over a piece of fruit? Would this man of great humor come down hard on someone who brought back the wrong color apple?

Letterman left without saying goodbye and all I could think was, "Huh...?" I never watched him the same way on TV again.

Jerry Springer

When television spiraled into a circus of chair-throwing, hair-pulling, fist-fighting, profanity-yelling, cross-dressing, sex-addicted guests, Jerry Springer was the ultimate ringleader. "The Jerry Springer Show" was so over-the-top when it debuted in September 1991 that security guards stood by on set and the opening featured a parental warning that stated the content may be inappropriate for children. With segments like "Sex Between Family Members" or "Nudists Talk About Why They Expose All," it gained a reputation for being the most sexually-explicit tabloid program.

So why not invite Springer on to dish about the show's 10-year success? If anyone had stories, Springer was loaded. Though maybe his material would be salty and I had to be prepared. In other words, I'd need to keep my finger near the "dump button" in case some raunchy words flew out of his mouth.

What I discovered was amazing. This guy, whose high-octane show could be jaw-droppingly raunchy and theatrical, was himself a charming and humble philosopher. Get a load of this personal history... British-born, Springer broke into American politics in 1971 as a city councilman and was forced to resign from office three years later after admitting to soliciting a prostitute. The following year, after owning up to his actions, he won the seat back by a landslide. In 1977, he was elected Mayor of Cincinnati and he served one term.

Springer was riveting, confirming the possibility that the best guests are often talk show hosts themselves. He could talk about anything and with heart. And without ever uttering a nasty word. He spoke most touchingly about coming to America on the Queen Mary with his parents when he was five-years-old. "In one generation," he said, "we went from the Holocaust to this wonderful privileged life I have today."

Who knew you could pluck a guest from the circus of tabloid television and discover the soul of a poet? Jerry Springer was multi-faceted and showed character. The qualities that anchored him were, perhaps, the very characteristics that allowed him to oversee his wacky show.

Jesse James

A major part of any satellite producer's job was to gobble up daily celebrity gossip pages such as People.com, *Page Six*, TMZ, and Perezhilton.com. These were my daily suggested four food groups. Back in 2009, a most unlikely Hollywood pair was Sandra Bullock and Jesse James.

Jesse James was star of the Discovery Channel series "Monster Garage" and a seemingly surly-mouthed, tattooed-ruffian who owned West Coast Choppers, an expensive motorcycle custom-design shop in Long Beach, California. His clients were bold-name rock, sports, and film stars. And now, he was married to his third wife - America's sweetheart, Sandra Bullock, who was known to regularly give million-dollar donations to natural disaster relief funds around the globe. This was her first and only marriage.

"How was it that they were a couple?" producer friends and I would dish while ingesting the latest gossip pages. Could this man with the tattooed arms, wild past, and three kids really settle into a life with Bullock, adopting babies in far-flung lands and hitting flea markets and antique shops on the weekends?

Meeting him made me see how it might work because he was extremely personable. In May 2009, James dropped by my studio for three hours as part of a media blitz to promote his Spike TV reality show "Jesse James is a Dead Man." In it, he performed death-defying stunts, the first episode drawing two million viewers, the largest audience ever for its genre.

This rough and tough "Mr. Bullock" was actually warm and fuzzy. By the time he went on-air and spoke about his career, he became a poet. "I use chrome and metal as extensions of my dreams," he said describing his work. "It's all art to me."

The media, I was convinced, was the root cause of his bad rep. Anyone who saw beauty in welding cold hard pieces together was a perfect mate for someone like Sandra Bullock. This so-called "bad boy" was a victim. Or, so I thought.

About four weeks later, while Bullock was on a media tour in Europe promoting her new movie "The Blind Side," multiple women came forth to say they had affairs with James during their five-year marriage. What followed was a public apology by James saying, "There is only one person to blame for this whole situation and that is me." Three weeks later, Bullock filed for divorce.

I was reminded, when you sit where I sit, you only get a snapshot into the whole story.

Paul Begala

When you sign on as a producer and work with a cross-section of celebrities and politicos, you quickly earn additional skill-sets - including those of part-time shrink. In this era of heated left-right talk radio (significantly weighted to the right), I had reason to believe that former Clinton advisor and Democratic political consultant Paul Begala suffered from a little paranoia.

At his request, Begala's publicist demanded a "personality profile" on each host he was scheduled to speak with on a satellite tour and I was taken aback. No one had ever asked for such a thing.

"All 22?" I asked with disbelief. "I'll be writing all night."

"You want to talk with Paul or not?" the publicist asked threateningly.

While creating a profile on each talk host late that night, I questioned why I was helping the "Crossfire" talking head sell his book, *Is Our Children Learning: The Case Against George W. Bush* (Simon & Schuster, 2000). Is he paranoid, arrogant, or both? Wasn't he one of the masterminds (along with wild-eyed caffeinated Cajun cohort James Carville) to usher Bill Clinton into the White House?

The next day, the interviews transpired without a hitch - not one conservative host gave him a tough time.

"You see," I joked with Begala afterwards, "loud-mouthed conservatives can be polite."

Silence. He said nothing. After an awkward moment, we said our goodbyes.

Later, I asked his publicist how was it that a man of his experience was so concerned about what would happen in the interviews that he requested a profile of each host.

"He wasn't concerned," she said, which for me translated as, "He *was* concerned."

"Okay," I responded, which translated as "I respect your loyalty to the guest... but I don't believe you."

"Whatever," she said dismissively.

Paul Begala, I concluded, projected a mild-mannered, Boy-Scout image on stage but was far more of a control-freak behind stage. What I came to learn about heavyweight politicians like him, they are *all* control freaks. Some more than others. I guess that's how they become heavyweight politicians in the first place.

"I'm outta here!"

Radio producers arrange door-to-door car service for a guest, fill the green room 'fridge with specialty requests for such things as imported ginseng tea, cranberry-almond trail mix, and pink champagne - but nothing guarantees that a guest will stay in the hot seat once the on-air light goes on.

Here are a few who got away - or tried...

Lewis Black

Comedian Lewis Black, who regularly performed at colleges and comedy clubs around the country, promised two hours of interviews during his busy schedule back in July 2006. He was flacking his latest book, *Nothing's Sacred* (Simon Spotlight Entertainment, 2005), a collection of rants against such things as cell phones, Starbucks, and religion - *all* religions.

At break two, about 20 minutes into the series of interviews, Black removed his headset, stood up, and politely addressed me through the mic, "Thank you... It's been great." Then he stepped toward the studio exit.

"Wait – WAIT!!!!" I shouted, as I eye-balled the countdown clock. "You're scheduled for another 90 minutes." I ran out of the control room and caught up.

"I've got errands to do before catching my plane later," he said, turning again toward the exit. Then over his shoulder he added, "Just send those first two interviews to all the others on the schedule."

"Mr. Black, that's not how it works. Each host expects a one-on-one. You must get back in the studio and finish."

We locked eyes.

"Errands such as *what*?" I asked, finally breaking the silence.

And that is why - over the next hour-and-a-half - I tracked down a pair of white Nike running sneakers in size

13 for delivery, called his local cleaners to drop off pressed pants to the studio, all the while sewing two buttons back onto his shirt.

A producer did what she must to keep the wheel oiled.

John Ashcroft

Not every guest who got antsy stayed within my clutches. But then again – how was a producer supposed to manhandle a former Attorney General of the United States?

In October 2006, John Ashcroft was out plugging *Never Again: Securing America and Restoring Justice* (Center Street, 2006). His rich place in history was chock full of heated talking points - including his lost Senate reelection effort to a deceased opponent, a bumpy transition through 9/11, decisions over the Hansen spy scandal and the execution of Timothy McVeigh.

The problem? The former Attorney General fell out of favor with a sizeable portion of the public. And as luck had it, his critics were calling into his interviews that day.

"How dare you hold prayer meetings in the American people's government office every day?" one caller chewed him out in reference to a 2001 *Washington Post* story that reported Ashcroft ran a Bible study in his office every day at 8:00 am.

"Shame on you for evading military service six times during Vietnam and then, years later, sending our boys to war," another reprimanded.

It was one hostile call after another. Could I really blame the nation's top law enforcer for getting up and walking out?

Yes.

I was a producer first. So when he rose from the chair in a huff, I lunged forward, hoping to shout him back into a sitting position.

"EXCUSE ME - Mr. Attorney General - where do you think you're going?" I asked, completely forgetting in the moment at whom I was hollering. You see, whenever an interview was going on, I had one boss and one boss only - the clock. And it was ticking… but not enough. We still had 50 minutes to go.

In retrospect, I can't blame him for wanting to escape. Why should he explain himself to inquisitors like "Joe from Minnesota?" But I gathered this high-ranking politico lived by different rules than most guests who came through the doors. He even came with the title "the Honorable Former US Attorney General John Ashcroft" which the publicist instructed I call him. He bolted for the exit and the closest he came to any words of apology were, "I'll make it up... I promise."

Whatever could that mean?

Three days later, I found out. Inside a tightly packed box from Washington, D.C. were a dozen copies of Ashcroft's book, all autographed on the title page. I dug inside for a note, but found none. Not even a breezy, hand-written scrap of paper saying, "Hey - sorry to cut it short, but..." Instead, 10 pounds of dead trees.

A politician like John Ashcroft might have been called a "public servant," but that didn't translate into being an engaging guest on talk shows.

Again, big-time politicians were often a pain in the ass.

Madeleine Albright

When former Secretary of State Madeleine Albright came in the studio one morning to tell stories from her recently-published book *Read My Pins: Stories from a Diplomat's Jewel Box* (Harper, 2009), she had every reason to be upset by what was about to transpire. I made a serious error in judgment that I regret to this day. Not only did I confirm Democrat Albright with hostile conservative hosts, I also booked her with "morning zoos" - shows hosted by guys named "Cowhead," "Pond Scum," and "Smelly Belly."

What made me do such a thing? I shortsightedly thought I was helping her sell books, so I simply figured the more interviews, the merrier - even if I set her up with arch-conservatives while she was clearly liberal. Besides, I thought, if this same woman can take on Iranian President Mahmoud Ahmadinejad, then clearly she was able to razz right back at loud "yakkers" with sixth-grade potty humor named "Straight Dope" and "Black Bean." It just seemed like a good idea at the time.

"What... sort of shows are these?" she asked, a troubled look growing on her face while holding up the list of shows I had set on the console before her.

My stomach dropped to my feet. I realized in that moment what a terrible mistake I had made. A hot wave of terror rose up my back.

"I'm here to talk about my book," she said, looking me straight in the eyes.

"Exactly," was what I said with a gulp. "Pins, not policy."

Uh-oh was what I was thinking.

Albright's book was loaded with colorful stories about heated moments she experienced during meetings with global figures, the kind that inspired her to "deploy" certain pins from her "arsenal of 300," as she referred to the broaches in her jewelry box. Take the famous standoff she had with Saddam Hussein in 1993 when he had called her "an unparalleled serpent." From that point forward, whenever she met with him or other Iraqi officials, she dug into her jewelry box for her gold snake pin.

Right out of the gate - the scheduled two-hour string of interviews got off to a rocky start when the first host introduced the Secretary of State in this way: "If we were to send more ugly old broads like our next guest to foreign countries, perhaps we could shock the 'Al- Qaedas' into submission." I went numb.

Thank goodness, she hadn't yet plugged her headset into the system so she was totally disengaged. While smiling at her through the glass, I screamed like a fiend into the talkback connection at the upcoming host, saying, "Hey - cut the nasty talk - or I'll cut you short." They knew that I meant it.

However, I still sweated through that first interview. When one of the crew made a sly dig about her "inevitable divorce with a puss like that" - the kind of comment I told them to lay off - Ms. Albright shot me a dagger-like look. During the first break, she asked me pointblank, "WHAT are you doing to me?"

"I'm trying to help promote your book to an audience you may not normally reach," I said trying to soften the heat. My good intentions carried little weight, considering the next hosts had names like "River Rat," "The Love Sponge," and "Squeeze."

She was fuming. As much as I begged "Pukehead," the producer of the next show, to lay off her, I guess he just couldn't help himself. Morning hosts will be morning hosts. I fed red meat to wild lions.

How do I explain the morning zoo culture to a former Secretary of State? Not that I got a chance. Madeleine Albright was done. The frozen expression on her face said it all. She got up and walked out. I was devastated.

Madeleine Albright made her point - without a pin.

Guests *you* want out of the hot seat

For a producer to survive interviews with divas, B-list celebrities, and celebrity wannabes, he or she had to develop a Teflon ego and allow all the bitchy, bogus, and biting behaviors to wash off.

Easily said.

Talk radio listeners and morning show hosts love reality show stars. One reason is that these un-ripened celebs are all heart and drama. Radio thrives on the highs, lows, tears, and torments.

Two of the more emotionally-packed and beloved guests to come to my studio were Ruby Gettinger, the Style Network's spirited Southern redhead who tipped the scale at over 700 pounds, and Fantasia, who won the third season of "American Idol" in 2004. Their colorful, life-altering reality show journeys soon morphed into memoirs, giving each a chance to circle back on the talk show circuit and promote their stories in hardcover and paperback. In *Ruby's Diary: Reflections on All I've Lost and Gained* (William Morrow, 2009), we read about Gettinger's daily war with food addiction and how she sought to lose 400 pounds. "American Idol" winner Fantasia Barrino walked us through her shame over growing up functionally illiterate in *Life Is Not a Fairy Tale* (Touchstone, 2005). It became a *New York Times* best-seller.

Both of these newbie-celebrities, officially billed by their first names, barely polished by publicists, oozed with life struggles and pain in every interview.

And then there were the guests who were downright nasty...

Omarosa

Just when I grew to cherish each and every reality show guest, along came Omarosa. During the Clinton administration, she was hired in Vice President Al Gore's office as Deputy Associate Director of Presidential Personnel. She didn't keep the job very long. Omarosa Manigault-Stallworth had quite a history of getting fired... long before Donald Trump sent her home from "Celebrity Apprentice."

As noted in *People,* "The former political appointee - who spoke glowingly of her White House days - was banished from four jobs in two years with the Clinton administration." A former White House staffer said of Omarosa, "Her job was 'scheduling correspondent.' She was supposed to respond to invitations received by Vice President Gore. But didn't do her job - and that got everyone else in trouble."

According to Cheryl Shavers, the former Under Secretary for Technology at the Commerce Department, where Omarosa worked for just several weeks in 2000, even after she was repositioned in yet another gig, "She was asked to leave as quickly as possible, she was so disruptive." Shavers added, "One woman wanted to slug her."

I completely understood the sentiment.

By the time Omarosa joined me on radio in 2009, she had already appeared on more than 20 reality shows (including "Surreal Life," "Fear Factor" and "Girls Behaving Badly"). One of the twists in her life - and the primary reason to bring her on as a guest - was that she had enrolled in divinity school at the United Theological Seminary in Ohio. In 2012, she was officially ordained a minister.

The interview she conducted under my watch was by a landline from her home in California. As we proceeded, she grew more and more irritated - with me, with the hosts - spewing insults during breaks. "These hosts are really stupid." "What a waste of time." And finally, "I don't know why I agreed to do this."

Each and every time she bashed someone new - that is, *my* people, the guys I worked with every day - my adrenaline soared. *Them were fightin' words!*

"If it's so bad," I suggested, "why don't you just hang up?"

At which point she flung the words, "You're a fucking moron." I flung an F-bomb back at her, the first and only time I ever did so with any guest.

"On second thought," I added, "I'll hang up first." Then I did. Of course, now I had to explain to the remaining hosts what happened. Some, like Bill Meyer at KMED in Medford, Oregon - one of the nicest, hardest-working hosts in the business - asked me on the air to tell the story.

"Omarosa was true to her reputation," I said, telling the timeline of events. "Ironically," I added, "she came to promote her book *The Bitch Switch: Knowing How to Turn it On and Off* (Phoenix Books, 2008), informing women how to locate their 'inner bitch.'"

Thanks Omarosa. You inspired me to find mine.

Dr. Laura Schlessinger

One challenge I faced as a talk show producer was accommodating special requests by upper-management in booking guests that they wanted to help. We had developed a well-oiled publicity machine on which to bullhorn an author, celebrity, or actor out to the public and the guys upstairs would often want to use it for their own social, business, or political purposes. This syndrome applied (and probably still does) to the entire business in general - not just my company at the time. An interesting case occurred in 2008 when my boss stopped by my cubicle to ask me to "do something nice" for Dr. Laura Schlessinger. I knew what was coming next.

"She's been a friend to our company, so please arrange some interviews for her to promote her new book." Then came the difficult part - "Whatever you do, be sure no one mentions...," then he leaned in and added with a wink, "*you know.*"

"You know" translated as "Nude Picture-gate," the incident that occurred back in 1998 when Dr. Laura's ex-lover posted naked photos of her on the internet at the height of her success. The same woman who described herself on-air as "My kid's mom," and whose website proclaimed her "The dean of morality," was the subject of a very risqué nude pictorial. Making matters worse (and public sympathy thin) was that her ex-lover, the press later exposed, was at the time of their affair, *married*.

This was trouble. How do you demand any sane-thinking morning show host to "ignore" the biggest (and juiciest) story about Dr. Laura and instead only focus on her book? They may promise, "Boy Scout's Honor," but could I trust them? What's a producer to do?

People have often asked me what it was I did, minute-to-minute, while an interview was unfolding on-air. On a "normal" day, I was most likely riding the volume controls of the on-air voices, scanning the internet to watch for breaking stories, while keeping an eye on the clock (so as to remind the host on-air that it's time to wrap) among countless other things.

On this particular day, behind the scenes, I was prompting, threatening, and schmoozing every upcoming interviewer in their own language. "Hey asshole, if you say a peep about those nude photos, you won't get to interview Madonna next week," I warned, pretending she was in the pipeline.

It was a complicated dance when working with interviewers who considered having a moral compass a sign of weakness. These guys were attracted to dirt like heat seeking missiles. I needed them. They needed me. And all I could hope was that they needed me more.

Here's where the Dr. Laura interview got tricky. She opted to do a phoner - that is, conduct the interview by landline instead of live in-studio. She was at her home in California, nearly 3,000 miles away. Seconds after we exchanged hellos, she insisted we set up "a live Yahoo chat," an instant-message software that allowed her to communicate with me during the interviews. I immediately knew she was going to be difficult when she chose to write the entire exchange in capital letters, which everyone knows is the IM-style for "yelling."

Dr. Laura: WHY DID YOU POSITION SO MANY INTERVIEWS BACK-TO-BACK?

Producer: Because the more we do, the more we promote and sell your book.

Dr. Laura: WHY ARE ALL THESE HOSTS LIBERALS?

Producer: Actually, they're not. Most are conservative.

(I left out the truth: *Hey Laura, even conservatives find fault with your opinions.*)

Then she came at me like an air traffic controller:

Dr. Laura: PLEASE SWITCH THE FIRST AND THIRD HOSTS WITH THE FORTH AND SEVENTH.

Little did she realize that behind the scenes, I was corralling these loud-mouthed gabbers from publicly roasting her, all the while she was directing me on who she preferred to speak with, and literally micromanaging my every move. Didn't she understand that these interviews were set up days, sometimes weeks, in advance? Didn't she know her own reputation - and the muscle it took to grease this tour of mighty-mouths?

Unbeknownst to Dr. Laura while she was interviewing with one host, I was pleading with the next to draw on their inner Boy Scout - "Please!"

With all the juggling and IM-chatter I shared with Laura, I was actually unable to listen to the interviews. However, I could peripherally monitor the tones of voices and over the years, I've learned that, if steady, it means those frisky morning jokesters were probably being polite.

One interview down and nine to go. Two down and eight to go - one leap of faith after another. When I got down to "five to go," Dr. Laura shot me an IM, "ARE YOU TRYING TO SET ME UP?" I had no idea what she was "shouting" about.

Dr. Laura was throwing a hissy fit and all I could do was - to quote the title of the very book she was promoting that day - *Stop Whining and Start Living* (Harper, 2008).

What I wanted to say was: *Lay off lady, I'm promoting your book, delivering thousands of listeners to you, while also wrestling behind-the-scenes with "the boys" so they don't mention those skank-ass photos of you on the internet.*

That's when I realized that the interviewer she was freaking over was doing a spoof - and on her. They had set up a phony female caller to ask Dr. Laura, "What should I do about my boyfriend who posted naked photos of me on the internet?"

I dropped the line to the show.

"Want to take a break?" I asked. "Or blast through the remaining 62 minutes?"

"Let's continue," she said, convincing me that this woman was tough... that she doesn't get headaches, *she gives them.*

On paper, Dr. Laura had the right constitution to succeed as a strong guest - self-directed, opinionated, and certainly feisty. In addition, because she's a host, she understood the pacing of conversation and how to tap into new ideas. Yet, these same qualities tortured me. For years, I avoided booking her because I sniffed out trouble. But fortunately we finished the interviews without further incident and I survived to tell the story. (I also owed a lot of favors to the hosts who interviewed her with uncharacteristic restraint that morning.)

With a guest like her, the lessons are many. I've often wondered if she used up all her favors along the way, if she burned through so many people on her rise to fame that no one helped her when the going got a bit rougher for her in the years that followed.

About two years later on her syndicated radio show, she ranted and spewed the N-word in response to a caller and stirred up so much negative news that she was subsequently self-pressured (not fired) off terrestrial radio. "N-Word-gate" forced her to reinvent herself on satellite radio, where she never recaptured her gigantic media profile.

Joan Rivers

"This run-down is too fucking crammed," the late Joan Rivers screamed at me through the talkback at 6:55 one cold, snowy morning in 2009.

An F-bomb? Before 7:00 am?

Joan goes down as the only guest who ever dropped one with me even before we said hello. All I could do was hope that the rest of the morning would go better.

"You're not giving me enough breaks between interviews," she bristled again. The E! Network star joined me this day to promote "Fashion Police," and now she was policing me.

"If you need longer breaks at any time, I'll accommodate," I yelled back. "Just trust me with this. I've been at this for years and know I can do it," I assured her. Which of course was my way of saying, *you may know a pleat from an appliqué, but I know a solid rundown from a dud.*

What I didn't tell her was that she and I shared a mutual friend. Instead, I waited.

Before long, she was yelling again - at a juncture when we still had an uncomfortable two hours to go.

"I've been meaning to tell you," I said, "your friend - and mine - David Bernstein says hello." David, a big honcho in the radio business, was at one point *her* boss, when she hosted a radio talk show at WOR in New York City. As a matter of fact, he was the one who *hired* her there.

She paused. It computed… hmmm, he's going to hear about her nasty attitude.

"David! David! What a guy!"

"Absa-tively," said I. Now we were buddies.

Media exhibitionists

Three kinds of guests have sat before the mic during my career as a producer. The first came with an agenda - to promote a book, TV show, movie, or political platform. These guests gained as much, if not more, by the exposure we provided as the shows did by having them on. After their appearance, I wouldn't hear from them again until, perhaps, their next project. They were the most common type of guest, usually fueled by a publicity machine that operated in a symbiotic relationship with the talk business. Bottom line, guests like these brought *something* of value to the table for the privilege of selling something specific.

The second type of guests - well, when lucky enough to land them - actually had nothing obvious to promote… and when they did, they were still choosy about the shows they would go on and difficult to book. You know them with names like Clinton, McCartney, Clooney, and Streep. These big-time newsmakers and celebrities operated above the fray, having no need for extra publicity. For them, I'd compose carefully-worded email after email followed by carefully-worded phone call after phone call (to schmooze and grease my luck) and hope to open the gate for delivery. Even producers on the big-time, late-night TV talk shows sweated over ways to coax such guests.

The third kind of guest was consistently entertaining and reached a level of fame that required only one ongoing product to promote - themselves! What did Donald Trump, Arianna Huffington, Dr. Ruth, Henry Winkler, and Kreskin have in common? They hardly ever said no to an interview request. And at one time or another, they each offered to be available at a moment's notice - whether to address a breaking story within their realm of expertise or to fill in for a guest who unexpectedly canceled.

They understood how the game was played and how to fully engage a host and audience. In a bind - I needed these "media exhibitionists" (a term coined by my husband to replace the more uncomplimentary, "media whores"). I kept their phone numbers fully secured in my speed dial. They were my "go-to" guys.

The one I called most often - who could speak to the latest Hollywood divorce or another childhood actor suicide - was none other than...

Danny Bonaduce

Best known for playing Danny in the 1970s TV series "The Partridge Family," former child actor Danny Bonaduce landed a whole other role in popular culture: lovable-yet-pathetic bad boy. Unable to land a long-term acting gig after the show ended in 1974, Danny became a regular guest on radio because he "out-zoo-ed" the so-called on-air talent by telling off-the-wall, self-deprecating real-life stories about his latest self-destructive act(s).

The car accidents! The bullying! The drunk and oversexed women! Such were some of the high-octane reports regularly featured in the daily newspaper as well as his on-air, gravelly-voiced rants about them. At heart was his own struggle with drugs and alcohol. Danny became radio's answer to "Reality TV" before the genre was conceived in its modern form.

The funny thing about him? Just when you think he exhausted all bad boy possibilities, he landed back in the tabloids. Eventually, he packed up these experiences in his autobiography, *Random Acts of Badness* (Hyperion, 2001)... which, of course, generated more bookings on talk shows.

One of the more unusual circumstances on reality television happened in 2005 on VH1 cable network's "Breaking Bonaduce" when he made headlines once again as the only "reality star" who ever attempted suicide on camera. *The New York Times* declared it "an excruciating excess of reality." When that attention died down (after a stint in a psychiatric ward), he drummed up more publicity through a 2007 televised boxing match with Barry Williams, who played his brother Greg on "The Brady Bunch." Danny eventually landed a radio show with former child star Mario Lopez (of "Saved by the Bell").

When it came to his personal life, one classic tale went something like this:

"One afternoon after partying hard the night before, I somehow managed to cross the threshold of another major turning point in my life. Upon waking up in bed, I asked the woman next to me, 'So, what's your name?'

"You know what she says? '*Mrs.* Danny Bonaduce.' I nearly fell to the floor."

He explained how he wooed her into bed the night before by promising to marry her. Pillow to pillow, face to face, she forced him to keep his word. Within days, they were official. That, he explained, is how he got married for the second time in his life.

After a third divorce, he unsuccessfully shopped around a reality show called "*The Next Mrs. Bonaduce*."

Never one to say "no," Danny landed on my short list of go-to "experts" whenever a dirty divorce emerged out of Hollywood (Tom Cruise to Katie Holmes, or Britney Spears to childhood friend Jason Allen Alexander, for example). On any of those breaking stories, Danny spoke with authority.

Chapter Sixteen
EXPANDING HORIZONS

One particular adventure in my career stands out above the rest. It gave me an opportunity to learn the difference between second-hand information versus first-hand experience in the larger world.

It began when an invitation came across my desk in March 2007 to fly to Israel (11 hours each way) and spend 96 hours collecting cultural factoids, political insights, general intelligence, and potential future guests for my work. The fact that I was considered influential enough even to be approached for this trip was indeed an honor. I jumped at the opportunity.

What kind of rocket is that?

Here's something I never expected to add to my resume: "Able to identify a Qassam rocket."

Thanks to the non-profit organization America's Voices in Israel, I embarked upon a jam-packed, five-day trip to the Middle East with a half-dozen other broadcasters to better understand the people, ancient history, modern-day culture, inventiveness, industriousness and, of course, years of conflict there. We were under no obligation to report any specific political point of view - our guides were confident that the facts we encountered would speak for themselves.

One stop was in the backyard parking lot of a police station in Sderot, a city that had been an ongoing target of rocket attacks from the Gaza Strip since 2001. It was there that I first encountered the gnarly, rusty remains of the deadly device.

About 25 pounds and as tall as a two-year-old, it was piled on a stack of about 100 others that had descended upon the community that past month alone. Designed by the military arm of Hamas, it tore through buildings - or left pockmarks on nearby walls and rooftops in ongoing attacks, sometimes as many as three or four a day. As I held this particular shell in my arms and posed for pictures, the air hummed with tension. I knew that this was one of many targeted areas I'd visit and that at any moment, life could be turned upside down. It mirrored the heightened emotion in New York City the weeks and months after 9/11 when pedestrians regularly looked skyward.

In Israel, that vigilant mindset was (and still is) the norm. Israeli citizens, Sderot residents in particular, were constantly on the alert thanks to a radar system that sounded whenever it detected a rocket overhead. Residents had 15 to 45 seconds to seek shelter before impact. That is, less than a minute to run. Visitors were always told to be aware of the closest shelter… and they were just about everywhere.

Almost all buildings in Israel - homes, hospitals, offices and schools - were designed with a cement shelter, usually below ground and large enough to fit 40 to 50 people. Behind the shrapnel-proof, reinforced steel door was a temporary home away from home, complete with multiple couches, foldout metal beds and mattresses. Even back in 2007, mobile phones were designed with apps that directed Israelis to the nearest secure area when they traveled in unfamiliar neighborhoods under sudden attack.

Welcome to El Al

Qassam rockets, air raid sounders, random attacks - by now, you may ask why an American radio broadcaster would want to put herself in such a tenuous situation.

That was one of the many questions El Al's security asked me during the screening process at Liberty International Airport in Newark, New Jersey just hours before boarding the flight - and at such a rapid rate that I hardly had time to think. This, of course, was precisely the idea.

"What's your mother's name?"

"Where was she born?"

"What about your father… his place of birth?"

"And you - where were you born?"

"What's your occupation?"

"What's your reason for travel?"

Though I had only just met this screener 10 minutes before, he knew more about me - my age, my mother and father's parents' names - than any of my colleagues would ever think or care to ask.

Later, I understood that he was not so much interested in my answers as he was in my attitude and tone, looking for anything suspicious. The Israeli guide and translator who drove us around the country told the story about a pregnant female passenger from Great Britain who, at the screening process, appeared to be the least likely candidate to carry an explosive. In fact, she was as innocent as she acted because, unbeknownst to her, it was later revealed that her husband, who boarded a separate flight, had been covertly partaking in plots against the country and secretly stashed a bomb in her suitcase.

Israel had been dealing with terrorism long before it became a common concept in American public consciousness and anti-terrorism became a worldwide industry. Violence against the Israelis had become normal occurrences. I will never know what inspired that first screener to send me to yet another set of agents for more questioning. After all, my fellow travelers - radio broadcasters who are known for scrappy attire and third-day-growth beards - somehow zipped right through. Next thing I knew, I was standing before two redheaded screeners about 30- and 35-years-old. What took me aback were their distinct Northern Ireland brogues. They were *Irish!*

Their questioning was virtually a repeat of the original screener's. When they seemed satisfied and gave me a ticket to join my colleagues, my journalistic curiosity could no longer hold back. How was it, I asked, that these two women came to work for El Al?

"Terrorism," the older-looking one answered, "is as familiar in Belfast, where I grew up, as it is in the Middle East." She reminded me that terrorism is terrorism is terrorism. Before sending me on my way she added, "When you get a moment, look up the birthplace of the sixth President of Israel, Chaim Herzog." Which I did - discovering the kind of factoid that a news producer would love. Herzog was born in Belfast, Ireland and had a full-fledged brogue himself. He served as President of Israel from 1983 through 1993.

Would you like to check your gun?

Eleven hours later, we finally landed in Israel. With whatever sleep I snatched on the flight, the screening process continued. This time, at the entrance of the Herzalia Conference Center where VIPs such as former-President Jimmy Carter and American attorney Alan Dershowitz - along with Israeli leaders including Benjamin Netanyahu - were among the attendees scheduled to speak about the politics, society, and security in the country. At the entrance, a female guard with intense coal-black eyes looked deeply into my bloodshot weary ones and asked at a rat-tat-tat pace, "YouCarryGun?" I'd never been asked such a question, nor in such a frenetic way, let alone carried or fired a gun. Taken by surprise, I asked her to repeat it.

But this time, she leaned in closer and scanned me with suspicion while also raising her voice an octave. That was my introduction to the constant intensity that filled the air in this tiny country the size of New Jersey. The rapid-fire speech pattern followed me wherever we went, whether in Hebrew or English, the two most-commonly spoken languages. That hyper-style language, I gathered, resulted from the Israelis' constantly pulsating hearts.

For a tiny country under constant threat, it was no surprise that every citizen - male and female - is called to serve in the Israeli Defense Force, (IDF). "All Israelis are soldiers," said a woman in uniform I met outside the Gaza Strip where many attacks originated. "We Israelis, one and all, are taught to fight back," she added, looking no older than 21 but sounding twice that age. "We are not victims." It was the same psychology that emerged in post 9/11 New York City - only on steroids.

That focused mind and the constant vigilance was what I noticed as I traversed the country with my colleagues, shuttled by our brilliant translator/driver/guide David Baradt, who himself was part of the full-scale mobilization in 1973 against Egypt and Syria, otherwise known as the Yom Kippur War. Like many other Israeli citizens, David operated as if he had radar imbedded into his head. While driving us through the countryside, he was alert, scanning the streets, buildings and horizon, looking out for, well, we-never-quite-knew-what. In addition to the obvious tourist attractions, he pointed out various locations where suicide bombers took Israeli lives - a corner bus stop, a popular Tel Aviv disco, and a shopping center. Once, when tangled in gridlock, David nonchalantly informed us that the bottleneck was not necessarily caused by traffic - but possibly police searching a car for a suspected bomb. It might have been just another day for this Israeli, but clearly a new dimension of the world for me to experience.

Being there

If I learned one thing on this trip, it was you can rip-and-read the latest international news story while sitting in the safe bubble of a newsroom, but it's an entirely different experience to stand at a tense border in view of the rubble. You wonder if and when a rocket may drop next, or a tunnel breaks open below your feet, bringing you face-to-face with an attacker.

Traveling north (some 84 miles) to Haifa, Israel's third-largest city, we met with the then-mayor Yona Yahav, who gave us a "tour of the town" while standing at his office window overlooking the city and beyond. He pointed to specific targets recently hit by Hezbollah bombs, lobbed across the northern border from Lebanon. How easy it was to see the Lebanese border - a mere 18 miles away. We understood the tension generated by how close these warring countries are situated side-by-side on the Eastern shore of the Mediterranean Sea.

During this whirlwind trip, I filed reports to my New York newsroom via the radio studio at *The Jerusalem Post*. That's where I got the warmest of welcomes by one of the local producer/engineers at the paper. "Mishpocheh," he greeted us - the Hebrew word for "family." It also implies the largest interpretation to that meaning. Or as I came to understand it on this day, family we just hadn't met yet.

No doubt, we saw ourselves in each other, despite the 5,627 miles between us. It's a familiar feeling I've had whenever in a newsroom outside the United States. Ideally, journalists are an army of do-gooders, seeking truth (whatever that is). In Israel, the country's survival depended on it. In a broader sense, the proper workings of any society depends on it.

During the 96 hours I was on land, I never regretted the intensity that came with such a trip. Why wouldn't I want to see-breathe-walk-talk the very experience that I produced-packaged-reported nearly every day for five years? That was the reason for this trip.

In the four full days I was there, none of the five attacks that occurred at random locations around the heated zones were ever mentioned in the American media. And that was likely because there were no casualties. Everyone knows, "If it bleeds, it leads… and if it doesn't bleed, who cares?" These skirmishes called up another day of courage, vigilance, survival, and faith among the citizens who live life on the front line.

I'm resigned to accept that I will never fully understand the seemingly endless conflicts in the Middle East. Regardless, I returned to the United States a more educated producer and a smarter human being.

Chapter Seventeen

THE POLITICS OF POLITICAL GUESTS

Rarely, if ever, in this post-9/11 world does a radio show welcome a President of the United States live and in the flesh on its own turf. More often than not, he (or really his handlers) will agree only to a phoner with the understanding that the scheduled time will likely be bumped (more than once) - and maybe even to the weekend. Complain? Never. Radio broadcasters consider themselves lucky to conduct an interview at any time with the POTUS.

When President Bill Clinton saw the power of talk radio (especially the muscle wielded by Rush Limbaugh), he and his team zeroed in on selected hosts who successfully rallied listeners into their "town halls of the airwaves." Some talkers were even invited to the White House (in reality, usually the nearby Executive Office Building) where he or she would conduct a pre-tape. (Even TV correspondents on shows such as "60 Minutes" set up these remote interviews, though somehow they always schmooze their way into the Oval Office. There you go - that's TV for you.)

The first and only time I participated in a presidential visit to a radio station was in 1983 when WOR-AM, New York hosted a former president live in studio. Jimmy Carter was on a publicity tour for *Keeping Faith* (Bantam Books, 1983), one of the 20-plus books he would eventually write after leaving office.

First came the Secret Service. Not everyday radio station visitors, I assure you.

Three days before the interview, the Secret Service's advance team showed up - a logistics agent and a technical security officer. This would be one of two visits before the official one with the former-Commander-in-Chief. We were instructed to stay put at our workstations during the former-president's arrival and departure - the most sensitive moments of any trip. Secret Service agents were positioned at various entrances and exits of the building - doors, staircases, and elevators - to ensure that each was secured.

We watched as this team examined ceilings, windows and other vulnerable points that represented potential targets from another building or floor. They scanned for explosives - including under the carpet. They checked all the closets. At one point, one of these men in black with his shiny special agent lapel pin requested that I clear out the closet nearest to the studio so that if "an event" did occur on the day of the visit, an officer could simply grab Carter and drag him inside.

I subsequently learned that during such presidential visits, the Secret Service also plots out routes to the nearest hospital, alerting them ahead of time before an emergency may arise.

Keep in mind, Carter had been out of office about three years at this point. Imagine what security operations buzz around a *sitting* president (especially after 9/11).

Looking back at the elaborate prep (not to mention, the danger), it is clear today why presidents choose phoners. Since the assassination of JFK in 1963, Americans have witnessed numerous attempts on presidents: two on Gerald

Ford (both in September 1975); one on Ronald Reagan (1981, when James Brady was wounded); and multiple threats against others. It surprises me today that President Carter even *considered* dropping by our studios in the heart of Times Square.

What I remember as well from the days preceding that visit were the numerous memos that came down from management ("Keep the area around your desk clear" and "No joking around with the Secret Service," for example). When Secret Service officers finally did show up prowling around our workspaces, it was the only time in my career that I ever witnessed anyone dusting the equipment. (At least 10 years of buildup was quite gunky.) This was also the only time I saw an engineer dressed in a shirt and tie.

When the former president finally arrived on site that day, all I saw were his right ear and the top of his head. It was impossible to see past my fellow producers and engineers who were craning their necks to peek through the parade of suited men who surrounded him like a fence. Even the way they walked in stride down the hall seemed choreographed right down to the step.

Since then, boy, have things changed - and not just for the president. I have seen similar security precautions and "Secret-Service-like" teams work for talk show hosts Rush Limbaugh and Glenn Beck. Before those guys stepped foot inside *TALKERS* magazine's 2008 and 2010 radio conventions, their handlers staked out the site days ahead.

It's getting hot in here

Every political season unleashes a predictable hurricane of editorials and ads while talk show producers around the country hunker down to brainstorm creative ways to present the whirlwind of campaigns in the weeks and months that lead up to Election Day. How, oh how, do TV and radio talk shows add pizzazz to the ongoing, often laborious, election segments? They go Hollywood!

Bill Clinton's saxophone-playing 1992 appearance on "The Arsenio Hall Show" was one of the glitziest break-through examples. In 2007, Arkansas Governor Mike Huckabee, a bass player, showed off his skill with his homegrown band "Capitol Offense" while on the campaign trail through Iowa, appearing at county fairs and on local morning radio shows. Since then, Barack Obama has enjoyed a 2011 and 2012 schmooze-fest with the ladies on "The View." Some call this the Hollywood-ization of Washington, DC. But try as they might, the candidates can't be everywhere. Instead, a conveyor belt of unexpected "experts" - a certain glitterati from Tinseltown - may step forward to discuss policy. Perhaps you know them by names such as "Dustin," "Brad," and "Angelina."

Prior to the explosion of social media, radio was the most accessible venue for candidates and their celebrity-proxies. If they wished to reach a particular geography of voters in the country, all they had to do was pick up a cell phone and dial in from wherever they happened to be. They could also conveniently target certain voter groups by researching the political bent of the hosts being contacted. The most attractive quality radio offered for the constantly challenged campaign coffer? It was free and an opportunity to run a political ad disguised as information and entertainment.

Handlers back at campaign headquarters knew if you wanted a concentrated audience of politically-driven fans, you turned to talk radio. It has owned politics for more than a quarter-century (thank you, Rush Limbaugh). Speaking of Rush and the power radio wields, who among us has forgotten his White House sleepover in the summer of 1992 mentioned earlier? A photograph that ran in newspapers across the country featured radio's grand Pooh-Bah with George H.W. Bush - the President of the United States carrying Rush's overnight bag into the White House for a stay in the Lincoln Bedroom.

Cher

The woman who once showed up at the Oscars dressed like a tarantula, donning a three-foot high headdress with sparkles and sequined fishnet stockings had occasionally morphed into a political pundit. In October 2004, her handler called from Malibu to offer her as a guest on the roster of conservative morning shows that I was producing at the time.

To my shock, larger-than-life Cher - who changed boyfriends as often as her hairstyle - was actually low maintenance. At least, for me. Her handler might have felt otherwise. Over the phone, I could hear Cher's directions to the woman who placed the phone call... "Heat up water for my tea, please," then, "Time for my berries," and "Turn up the air, please."

While having a mega-star such as Cher in studio was always my first choice, "phoners" allowed a producer to eavesdrop on the star's true character during the commercial breaks. I once overheard a guest (known publically for his calm demeanor) go ballistic on his wife just as I called in for the interview. The doorbell rang, the dogs began yapping insanely, as she desperately tried to get her husband's attention because she had left home without her keys, creating a kind of "reality show" moment.

This hour-long interview with Cher exposed her fiery side. Citing her fear of the election, she abruptly ended her European tour to help her friend John Kerry "kick George W. Bush out of the White House." She added, "It's time to return America back to a kinder, gentler nation."

This very lively Cher explained how she was compelled to take an absence from "Living Proof: The Farewell Tour," a concert that grossed $250-million over the previous four months. Her heart, she said, "weighed heavy with worry over the possibility of another four years with George W." She urged listeners to "think with your heads and vote with your souls."

We learned that morning that the then-62-year-old diva had also worked for Jimmy Carter and Al Gore on their campaigns. And that some of her "best friends" (including at least one ex-husband) were Republicans.

While Cher never mentioned her ex- by name, we knew she meant US Representative Sonny Bono of California. Unexpectedly, she name-dropped another attention-getting Republican, or at least someone she identified as Republican (who actually was an Independent) - her friend, Lou Dobbs. The CNN anchorman had himself become headline news over the years for his anti-immigration rants.

"So wait - *what?* You're friends with him?" asked one of the hosts.

"He and I have been personal friends for years," she said. "He's someone I call regularly to debate issues. We get at it every few weeks or so."

Then, after a pause, she sighed and added, "Frankly, I don't respect either party. I just think Republicans are worse."

Michael J. Fox

By the time the then-45-year-old Michael J. Fox was stumping for John Kerry, he had been living with Parkinson's disease for over 10 years. Diagnosed in 1991, the actor went public in 1998 and soon after cut back on television appearances. The Canadian native, who had become an American citizen four years earlier, already had lobbied before Congress hoping to convince House members to overturn President Bush's limit on stem-cell research.

Missing from television for about six years, he took that plea to the public in the form of a television ad you can still see on YouTube. No one could have predicted the layers of controversy it stirred up, thanks to its stark message: "John Kerry strongly supports stem cell research. George Bush is putting limits on it. Stem cell research can help millions of Americans whose lives have been touched by devastating illnesses. George Bush says we can wait. I say lives are at stake and it's time for leadership. That's why I support John Kerry for president."

What took viewers by surprise was Fox's unexpected delivery. His tremors and uncontrolled muscle movements were so alarming for a public that hadn't seen him on television or in movies for years that some even questioned his authenticity. One such skeptic was Rush Limbaugh, who publically stated on his radio show that Fox "was either off his medication or acting."

Limbaugh told listeners, "He is exaggerating the effects of the disease. He's moving all around and shaking and it's purely an act. This is really shameless of Michael J. Fox."

This spiraled into a battle of words between Rush and Fox, which of course spilled out into newspaper columns and op-ed pieces, as well as perfectly-produced debate segments on radio and television. Rush argued that the Democrats exploited Fox's illness and that this was a ploy bound to backfire... all of which evolved into more GOP ammunition and questions about how the Democrats were running their campaign. Debates brought on more debates - beyond issues of stem cell research. It was messy.

Controversies were falling from the sky. Producers like me were happily benefiting from the non-stop, broiling conversation. It didn't even matter if we had celebrity or big newsmaker guests - the issue had legs all its own. This was "producer-heaven."

Whether Rush was acting in bad taste or simply telling an uncomfortable truth, I do not really know... although I thought about it for years. I had booked Michael J. Fox on several radio shows during that period but they were phoners and it really was hard to tell how much impact the disease had on him just from the sound.

George Clooney

"Before we confirm this," snarled the fastest talking, angriest woman I ever spoke with over the phone, "whatever you do, you do *not* ask George about his girlfriend. Clear?"

"Clear," I responded to George Clooney's publicist, my hand nervously tapping my desk calendar. A moment later, Clooney, one of the choicest celebrity "gets" of that era, was inked in. This was guaranteed bragging rights with friends and family for weeks.

Before we hung up, the publicist demanded a review, "What topic will you avoid - so help you God?"

"The girlfriend," I barked back.

Then she hung up. And for the first time in four minutes, I took a breath.

Yet, I had one glaring concern. *How do I convince uncontrollable morning talk show hosts to stay on topic, the Presidential election, and ignore you-know-what?* Their brand of radio was nicknamed "morning zoo" for a reason.

My only ammo was to threaten them in this way: "If you even think about asking George Clooney about his GF, you will suffer grave consequences - I promise!" (Which they knew translated as temporary suspension from future celebrity guest interviews.) And during "the season," those were loaded with A-tier names.

On the morning of the George Clooney tour, I reviewed the rules with each, zeroing-in on hosts such as "Pig Breath" and "Puke." I needed them to respect the "blacked out" topic.

Then the moment of truth: George called in directly to the control room as scheduled (his phone number blocked). I dialed the publicist into a listen-line so she could hear the interview for herself. Then I funneled George through to the hosts and crossed my fingers. Shortly thereafter, George was sharing his talking points about a Kerry White House and I began to breathe again. About five minutes in, even "the handler" sounded calm, as evidenced from an occasional "mmmm" that only I could hear through the overhead speakers.

My heart stopped, though, when "Pig Breath" chimed in with, "Hey George... two more minutes on Kerry and then we're going to want to talk about your recent movie... We're going easy on you." George laughed and like the cool guy he was, continued on his mission.

"John Kerry is a man of the people..." he said. "John Kerry will take a woman's rights seriously," he continued. "In fact, John Kerry has even gotten the attention of..." and then the dreaded words, "my girlfriend..."

Worse, he *named* her. At which point, I almost fainted.

The publicist went ballistic, screaming at me through the overhead speakers, the glass in the studio rattling. Sounding like a human air raid, she demanded that I "yank him off ...and now."

"BUT-BUT-BUT - *HE* did it – *HE* DID IT!" I shouted back at her through the talkback. "*He* brought up her name..."

"Get. Him. Off. Now." she squawked.

"Please..." I pleaded.

"OFF! Now!"

I surrendered.

While I never heard from George or his publicist again, I did read in the gossip pages that the Clooney household was having a fundraising event for John Kerry. All I needed to do was spring for the $1500-a-plate opportunity to possibly continue the conversation. (I later learned he raked in over $8-million.)

Joe Biden

When a major candidate who was running for president asked to be a regular guest every Monday for the length of his campaign, what was a producer to say? The answer, of course, was "Yes." Little did I realize, US Senator Joe Biden (D-Delaware) found his perfect medium - talk radio. The then-senator liked to talk. A lot.

To quote former-NBC news anchor Brian Williams, Biden suffered with "uncontrolled verbosity" and had a tendency to be a "gaffe machine." (As time eventually proved, Williams was one to talk!) At one point during the Biden campaign, Williams asked publicly, "Would Biden have the discipline you would need on the world stage?" That stinging comment made the rounds on the Sunday morning chat shows and served to prepare me. I was less worried about the global stage than the radio one.

In 2007, US Senator Joe Biden was the first of eight aspirants running for the Big Seat whose camp actually responded to my email (make that, multiple emails) requesting that he'd be a guest on talk radio. Hillary's camp completely ignored me.

Senator Biden, or "Joe" as he invited me to call him, was extremely radio-friendly. He had already proven this having announced his intentions to run for president in December 2004 on radio... specifically on "Imus in the Morning." (This was not his first try - he had run a 1988 campaign, but withdrew after a controversy that emerged over a failure to credit a speech written by another candidate.)

Joe was likable, very regular-guy-ish. Delaware voters must have thought so too since they elected him into the Senate, where he thrived since 1972. The state's largest paper, *The News Journal*, featured a January 23, 2006 column by Harry F. Themal saying, "Biden occupies the sensible center of the Democratic party" and then further praised his platform. "He plans to stress the dangers to the security of the average American, not just from the terrorist threat, but from the lack of health assistance, crime, and energy dependence on unstable parts of the world."

How wonderfully succinct were these "talking points." If only Biden were so concise when he opened his mouth. The joke behind the scenes? "If you ask him what time it is, he'll tell you the history of the clock." One sentence led to another and another. My job became managing his verbosity so to keep my real boss, the clock, happy.

"You only have six minutes in this next segment," I outright lied to him to build myself an extra cushion of time to hit the mark. Unfortunately, that did not always work. During one interview, as the clock ran down and my blood pressure up, the emotional senator was describing in detail how nearly three decades earlier, when just nominated to the Senate, his young wife and one-year-old daughter were killed in a car accident.

How does a producer interrupt *that*?

"…for five years I was a single parent with two sons…" he said, describing his sudden launch into single-parenthood. "I was a regular on Amtrak, commuting back and forth between the nation's capital and Delaware every weekend. I knew the conductors by name - some were my constituents."

I signaled into his earpiece to exit. But Joe kept going.

So I got louder into the talkback, "We're late. Out, please."

Still nothing. As we overshot a must-hit transition, I negotiated my way out of the original commitment and immediately prompted him via earpiece, "Joe. Please. Out!"

At which point, I gave up and bumped the next interview. My only resort was to speed-dial the only person who would understand. I called Joe's campaign manager in Washington, DC who sat like a loyal beagle outside his office. I begged him to march in and interrupt the senator who was still yapping.

"Break through the door and disengage him from the mouthpiece. Please..." I pleaded.

Clearly, this was not the first time the campaign manager ran interference.

"Now you know why he loves you radio people - the leash is longer than television."

"How do you deal with this all the time?"

"Lots of apology notes..."

Before long, I didn't have to worry about fighting the clock with the senator. He dropped out of the race on January 3, 2008, after capturing less than 1% of the vote in the Iowa caucus. Seven months later, he emerged as Democratic nominee Barack Obama's running mate. And the rest, of course, is history.

Mike Huckabee

You can take the candidate out of the radio station - but you can't take the radio out of the candidate. Mike Huckabee was obviously enthralled by the art of audio media. Once upon a time, long before the minister-turned-governor-turned-Fox-host became a presidential candidate, he was a news and weatherman on radio. Well, more precisely, a weatherman-boy. At the tender age of 14, "Huck" was dispatching bulletins and forecasting storms at KXAR in Hope, Arkansas.

So, when I shot his camp an invitation to do radio, they responded immediately. The same day! That enthusiasm translated into a standing interview every Thursday at 8:00 am for nearly four months (when his campaign folded).

True to his radio background, "Huck" was never late, usually calling in by phone from somewhere on the campaign trail, and knew how to hit the 10-minute mark perfectly. In other words, he was a "radio rat" who happened to be running for president.

What separated him from most other candidates on and off mic? His ability to be a "regular guy." Even more so than Joe Biden. While doing a mic check with me during the minute before going on air, "Huck" would gab like I was his buddy. I heard about the celebs he met in the green room the night before on Jay Leno or Letterman, or, more often than anything, "how hard it is to keep the weight off while on the campaign trail."

Before ever *running* for president, he actually was a *runner*, that is, to lose weight. In fact he ran four marathons, including one in 2005 - "...when I challenged and beat

Iowa Governor Tom Vilsack by 50 minutes, crossing the finish line at 4:38:31."

"You must be good," I complimented the 50-plus-year-old "recovering food-aholic" (his phrase) for coming in at that time.

"Used to be," he corrected me. "*The New York Times* once described my 110-pound weight loss as being so fast that it was as if I 'unzipped a fat suit and stepped out.'" Unfortunately, he said, he'll have to re-read the book he authored, *Quit Digging Your Grave with a Knife and Fork* (Center Street, 2005). While on the campaign trail, he felt his thin suit bulking up. History has shown that "Huck" went on to continue being weight-challenged.

Lessons of the Huckabee radio campaign were many. While he never made it to the White House, he did capture the public's heart, partially thanks to his one-on-one, average-man-on-the-radio way. And it paid off, as evidenced by his political star blazing a path into a future in television and radio... and subsequently another shot at the White House for 2016. Some could argue he failed upwards. His combined salaries from shows on Fox television and ABC Radio Networks definitely brought home a heftier salary than that of a US president.

Ralph Nader

When Ralph Nader stepped off the elevator on the third floor of United Stations Radio Networks, his knockoff London Fog raincoat and matching tan fisherman-like hat totally threw me. He appeared more like my Uncle Joe on the way to the Hudson River to throw a line than a future President of the United States. He was most definitely the only presidential candidate I've ever met who could hide in full sight - not a "handler" or press secretary orbiting about him. He was "Ralph," solo and carrying his own umbrella.

He removed his hat, extended his hand to introduce himself with his down-to-earth appeal and we walked into the studio. I couldn't help but notice his scruffy-looking black shoes. This same man who ran for President of the United States five times (twice each on both the Green Party and the Independent Party, and once as a write-in candidate) oozed a down-to-earth "average-ness."

As the interview unfolded, those shoes became the focal point of what some would consider his appeal - and why, he said, he should be elected president. A child of Lebanese immigrants, he was proud of his frugal upbringing and current lifestyle - a trait he said he'd bring to the White House if elected. "These shoes are the last pair of 36 I purchased from the army surplus store when I left the service in 1959. The price was so good, I bought three-dozen."

Then he said of his opponent, "Al Gore changes his clothes three times a day, and he has absolutely no idea who he is." He launched into talk about character-building and protecting the public from corporate greed - a philosophy resonating with his 1960s mission and best-selling book, *Unsafe at Any Speed* (Grossman Publishing, 1965), that appealed for federal car-safety standards to prevent accidents and protect passengers.

Though a man without "handlers" to carry his umbrella, he did have an army of supporter-friends who came on air to campaign for him, including documentary-maker and director Michael Moore, Patti Smith, and Phil Donahue.

From that standpoint, Nader was far more than a colorful "third-party candidate" for the presidency, most of whom get very little time on talk radio or any media attention for that matter. He was a major news/talk radio celebrity guest who had his own solar system of high-profile satellites orbiting around him throughout the campaign season. Further proof of the fact that the horsepower any individual brings to talk media as a guest is measured by a lot more than just their position or credentials.

The warriors of hate

Welcome to the dark side of booking a show - guests who *hate*. Or are, at least, *accused* by enough critics as "haters" so as to put them in their own special category. Stoked by the political season, and rarely quiet when it's over, these giants on the guest circuit were constantly at war with somebody, or really anybody. Many radio producers wondered, *are these people possessed?* The only thing these "hate warriors" seemed to love was a good fight. On the few occasions when they felt they've crossed the line of decency, they may-may-may say, "I'm sorry," or another popular statement, "I was just joking." Or, worse, "I was just exaggerating to make my point." Their hate talk was like a sport for them.

Somewhere along the line, they must have learned that "hate" created a buzz, captured a headline, and then sold more books… and you know what they were doing "all the way to the bank."

Just because I booked them didn't mean I felt good about it. Warrior-entertainers were always in demand and my job was to answer that demand, keeping the conversation bouncing and the talk show hosts happy.

They stirred up rage, as well as conversation and ratings. On days like that, my conscience weighed heavy and work was, well, work. Was I contributing to the problem by adding more fuel to the so-called hate talk?

Yes. No. Maybe. I often felt conflicted. Still do.

The guest who shall go *nameless*

Every time I booked this one particular female guest, I promised myself, "Never again!" By the fourth time I welcomed her into the studio, the intern just rolled her eyes at me. I wanted to slink away and managed to say, "Look, her books sell - she's on 'Politically Incorrect' tonight, Leno tomorrow.... She's in demand." I could not hide. I was a sell-out and knew it. Worse, everything this guest said left me feeling toxic.

On the surface, she was polished, polite, and never late. If only she were snippy or surly. She dressed well and knew how to schmooze the crew and hosts, and she never gave anyone reason to ban her. Even liberal hosts were charmed and fought to book her for return trips.

That is, until she stepped in doo-doo and philosophized about the motives of 9/11 widows. "These broads are millionaires, lionized on TV and in articles about them, reveling in their status as celebrities and stalked by grief-arazzis. I've never seen people enjoying their husbands' deaths so much," she said.

Her outrageous statement, said more than once on her book tour, went viral, inspired op-ed pieces in newspapers around the country and kicked off debate topics on nationally televised talk shows. The crazy thing - her philosophies had a life of their own. Radio producers no longer needed to book her. We simply handed over the related talking points - her latest crazy statements - to the hosts whose listeners called in outraged and in need of venting, or egads, throwing her their support. The show would explode with debate and ratings. Unfortunately, (and what pained me most), by doing so we helped her sell more books.

How did she have the gumption to say and write the things she did? She was once quoted in the *Washington Monthly* as saying, "I am emboldened by my looks to say things Republican men wouldn't."

So why book someone who was filled with such venom? By the time her fifth book shot up the bestseller lists around the country, I had had it. Really.

It's why I don't even mention Ann Coulter's name here.

Lou Dobbs

Google the then-CNN anchor Lou Dobbs and you'll uncover a recurring portrait. He's a grouch. Former colleagues and employees contributed gazillions of pages online with their own negative stories. Even his books were belligerent, the titles shouting off the dust jacket. The one that brought him onto my satellite tour early one morning was *War on the Middle Class: How the Government, Big Business, and Special Interest Groups Are Waging War on the American Dream and How to Fight Back* (Viking Adult, 2006).

What made him an interesting guest at the time (in addition to his many accomplishments) were the rumors bubbling up online, on talk shows, and through the producer-mills that Lou Dobbs was going to run for president. He was the anti-immigration watchdog who fumed and bristled instead of spoke when he discussed the "war on terrorism." He took on the future President of the United States and publicly questioned his birth certificate. (Free speech, yes! But, the decibels on the anger counter were reaching new heights.)

Dobbs was well-known inside the company where I worked, United Stations Radio Networks (USRN). He hosted four daily, one-minute financial features, which ran hourly between 5:00 am and 8:00 am. So given that relationship, his scheduler at CNN gave USRN first dibs for his radio interviews. He agreed to join us by phone.

Originally, Dobbs committed to two hours. But after many more requests flooded in, he approved extra time. First an additional hour, then an additional two. Finally, we settled on four hours one day and an additional 90 minutes the next. You could say he was in demand.

Having already heard outright horror stories about him from colleagues who produced his pre-dawn financial features, I was relieved he committed to an over-the-phone tour, not a live-and-in-studio one. The dirt I had uncovered about him on my Google research was enough to make me guzzle a bottle of Tums. Granted, I also uncovered a few tender details… his 99-year-old mother lived and was cared for in his home, and his wife's parents also moved onto the property, though in separate quarters.

By the time he joined me on-air, I understood that he wasn't just a television anchor, but (as he commonly described himself) an "advocacy-journalist," that is, someone who purposely offered a non-objective viewpoint because he believes in (and acknowledges) a social or political agenda. A more street-smart description comes from Kurt Anderson who wrote about Dobbs in *New York Magazine*, saying he was "mainstream media's first real anchor-rabble-rouser hybrid… a tail wagging the CNN dog."

Many journalists criticized his taking the "advocacy" route, arguing that it wasn't journalism, but rather an excuse to "sensationalize issues without objectivity." Another word for this practice is "propaganda." For example, Dobbs had no problem calling the "war on terror" the "war on Islamists" or question Barack Obama's birthplace. Apparently, many viewers and listeners loved this, as evidenced by the soaring book sales and ratings spikes in his CNN show.

Another telltale sign in his popularity at the time Dobbs joined me on the satellite tour - grassroots organizations around the country were calling for him to run for president. And that can feed any ego, I'm sure.

On the morning of his book tour, Dobbs connected with us by ISDN - again, technology that allowed a remote guest to sound live in studio, rather than distant over a tinny telephone. I did my usual mic check.

"Good morning, Mr. Dobbs - how about a count from five?"

Instead of descending numbers in return, he blasted a firing squad of words through the talkback: "PUL-Leeeeease, young lady, turn down that volume!"

"Gotcha," I barely stuttered out.

Recalibrate, I coached myself. *This job ain't about liking the guest, as much as it's about keeping him happy.*

Little wonder I went home exhausted some days. Working with this sort of talent was a mental ping-pong game. I resorted to schmoozing his ego.

"Mr. Dobbs, what you're hearing is my enthusiasm."

After a pause, his gruff voice boomed overhead, "Keep the enthusiasm, just turn down that volume. And by the way, you can call me Lou."

"Gotcha... Lou," I said, taking a deep breathe. *Okay - we're "friends,"* I thought.

The fact was, the Google search I had done during the preceding days warned me plenty about this abrasive, anchorman-grouch. It took 30 seconds and he lived right up to his reputation.

What made the experience further challenging were the two engineers within earshot that same morning.

"Eleven," one blurted loudly.

"Naw," the other piped in. "Fourteen."

They were placing bets on how many times Dobbs would snap at me through the talkback. Engineer number one worked regularly over the years on Lou's morning financial reports and spoke with experience.

He stuck his head inside my studio and said, "Try working with Lou when he was attempting to quit smoking. He used to smoke eight or 10 cigarettes an hour." Then he went on to describe how, as an audio engineer, he'd not only dealt with the outbursts, but also the sounds of long breathy drags on a cigarette he'd later have to edit before sending out the reports.

The other techie, who was a vacuum for gossip, reported that he had witnessed four producers in total quit the show in two years. "One even left in tears," he said. "The next day she crawled back asking to be rehired but was directed to leave. Lou skewered her on the way out saying, 'You don't belong in my foxhole.' At which point she again broke out in tears."

Why put up with a talent like this? He was a hot commodity. At least at the time.

I played the producer game and survived. Dobbs was Dobbs, authentic to whom he was. And he was a big "get." Little did I realize that 10 months later, I'd be sitting across from him in his office at CNN, interviewing for the executive producer position on a radio show he was about to launch with USRN - and that I'd land the gig.

Chapter Eighteen

IT'S ONLY A JOB INTERVIEW

When I stepped into Lou Dobbs' CNN office at 11:00 am on Tuesday November 20, 2007, the first thing I noticed was that he was physically way too large for his desk. And even his chair for that matter. Lou Dobbs was not just a television anchorman. He was the Hulk, casting shadows on the furniture. He appeared much bigger than his 6'2" frame described in TheAtlantic.com, one of the many profiles I had Googled before that morning's job interview.

Arlene Forman, his right-hand person, escorted me into his office and announced my arrival. Even while we stood at the door staring at the back of his head, he said nothing, fixated by whatever it was on his computer screen. She signaled with a nod for me to sit on the orange-tweed couch opposite his desk. And there I sat - stiff and silent. I faced Dobbs' back. He faced his computer monitor. I waited.

A summit meeting was unfolding in my head. Meet *The Girls:*

Bitchy Me: How many other producers sat in this very spot - getting the job, quitting the job, crying over the job?

Diva Me: This is insane. He hasn't even said "hello" or turned his head to acknowledge me.

Smarty-pants Me: Maybe this *is* the job interview. Maybe he's hoping to intimidate me, a kind of screening-out process.

Girl Scout Me: I bet that's it - and you'll just show him, won't you? Just keep smiling.

Diva Me: If you land the job, you'll be executive producer on a new talk show with a celebrity host and a nice paycheck. Not too shabby, a chance of a lifetime.

Girl Scout Me: YES! A salary bump...

Bitchy Me: What's with his attitude? He still hasn't turned around. All those blogs you read online say he's crazy. Well...?

Girl Scout Me: Land the job, pay the rent and plan Paris for the fall.

Bitchy Me: Of course, you could get up and leave right now. Just leave.

Girl Scout Me: Come on, girls. This interview is an opportunity to grow.

My attention shifted from "The Girls" to sneak a peek at my cell phone. The time now read 11:04.

What kind of game was this?

Not a muscle on his neck twitched, despite the fact that he definitely had a big head, a detail a producer friend once pointed out about anchormen in general. "Seriously, take a look," she said. "Ever notice how most of their heads are larger than what is proportionate to their bodies?"

Another subject for argument - at least on Gawker.com - that I analyzed while passing the time was Dobbs' hair color. One observer online described it as copper-grey;

another as molasses-brown. From my perch on the couch about four feet away, it was more a strawberry-blond over a halo of grey. (Or, as I later discovered, this was *that* week's color.)

This was a ridiculous way to spend the first six minutes of an interview.

Following the line of sight down from his head, I noticed the bulk of shoulders compacted into his navy suit and remembered the article I had read earlier that morning mentioning that he'd played football the first two years he was a student at Harvard - starting in 1963 - only to be sidelined after a knee injury.

All related, Girl Scout Me piped in. *Now he tackles immigration-related issues and kicks corporate America around, among others.*

I was fidgety. This was annoying. I waited. And waited more… It was 11:07.

Silence still.

While Dobbs was still bewitched by whatever was on his computer screen, I glanced over his shoulder at the stunning view. Opposite me was an entire wall of glass. He didn't have a *window's* view of Central Park, he had an entire *wall's* view. The traffic below orbited around Columbus Circle, and I imagined myself parachuting onto it. Any place but where I sat.

Next, I "title-hopped" along the bookshelf, mostly books he'd written: *Independents Day: Awakening the American Spirit* (Viking Adult, 2007); *War on the Middle Class: How the Government, Big Business, and Special Interest Groups Are Waging War on the American Dream and How to Fight Back*

(Viking Adult, 2006); *Exporting America: Why Corporate Greed Is Stripping American Jobs Overseas* (Business Plus, 2004); and *Space: The Next Business Frontier* (Pocket Books, 2001) among others.

And then he moved.

A real bastard

Lou Dobbs spun about in his chair, faced directly into my eyes, and leaning toward me, said, "I'm a real bastard. What do you think about that?"

I did not blink. I did not breathe. I went into automatic and said, "So I've heard. And you won't be the first I've ever had to work with."

So began the interview.

They say you can tell a lot about a person in the first 30 seconds of a conversation. That mini-exchange set the tone for the next six months of my career.

But wait - I'm getting ahead of myself.

The actual interview, or at least the parts I remember, hopscotched from politics to guest suggestions to books I'd read, all the while the "Summit Meeting Girls" sat silently by… *most of the time.*

Dobbs: Your immediate boss at USRN is a staunch liberal. Where do you stand?

Me: I'm a registered Independent… only recently. Not because of you, though, with all due respect. I converted from Democrat to Independent after reading Bernie Goldberg's book, *Bias*.

I was referring to *Bias: A CBS Insider Exposes How the Media Distort the News* (Regnery Publishing, 2001), which had made a big impression on me.

Me: I had also worked at CBS and thought he was onto something. All of which got me thinking about my politics.

Like throwing a knuckleball just after a fastball, he switched tactics.

Dobbs: What do you think about the new Chairman of the Armed Services Committee?

Diva Me: *Ah-ha, a trick question… He wants to see if I'm following the moves in the Senate.*

Me: If you mean Michigan Democrat Carl Levin, he's a great guest.

Dobbs: Carl Levin is an AWFUL guest. Just because someone's a senator doesn't mean they're good.

Girl Scout Me: *Note to self - not a good guest. Goodbye executive producer job.*

I was Mary Tyler Moore to his Lou Grant, caught in an awkward sideways-moving tap dance.

Me: I guess it depends on what you mean by 'good.'

I'll remember that.

Dobbs: Tell me your thoughts about guests for the first week of the radio show.

Me: With the primaries a few months away, we couldn't have picked a better time to kick off a radio show. We'll have guests climbing out of the walls - guests such as these...

At which point I passed him a two-page list of ideas and paused as he scanned the names and topic suggestions. It was 11:13 am.

He started looking over the list.

At 11:15, he was still looking at the list, analyzing every line, muttering to himself. It felt like an eternity.

Me: ...of course there's always the challenges facing education today and issues connected with jobs overseas.

Girl Scout Me: *That's right - drive home topics from his own books!*

He continued to scan the guests I had collected on the single-spaced page, an eclectic bunch whom I had booked on satellite tours, so I knew first-hand they were engaging personalities. But more important, they included many who hadn't yet made it to mainstream media. I knew that he knew that I was a quirky, yet independent, producer-type who scored some oddball "talking heads" by scouring offbeat sources and local newspapers. It was all there for him to see:

Todd Bensman, intelligence analyst and investigative reporter for the *San Antonio Express-News*, who wrote regularly about Iranian cells moving to and training in Latin America, then crossing Mexico into Texas.

Shannen Rossmiller, who had been conducting online investigations of Jihadist cells, bomb plots and extremists from her home in Montana, where she has been a mother of three. In the time that she was bed-ridden with an illness, she got her mind off the pain and into recovery by learning Arabic, and then intercepting threats that led to convictions in the United States.

Jim Meigs, editor-in-chief of *Popular Mechanics*. Meigs wrote regularly in his publication about the outsourcing of American jobs overseas and why they will survive and thrive there.

Dobbs prowled through the guest list, asked me about one or another, how or where I'd found them, and like the slow moving traffic in the city street below, I wondered where all this was going. It was 11:29.

Bingo!

Next thing I knew, Dobbs stood up and said, "Let's kick-start a radio show!"

I blinked.

Girl Scout Me: *You got the job. He just told you - YOU GOT THE JOB!! Jump up and shake his extended hand.*

When it all finally registered, I stood up to shake hands with the Hulk, reaching from across his desk. The Girls, one and all, were applauding.

But instead of walking out the door happy, my insides locked up. I sensed trouble ahead.

It was two days before Thanksgiving and yes, I was grateful for the salary boost. But deep down inside, I felt ill.

"Arlene, walk her to the elevator please," he said boisterously, my cue that it was time to leave. Before I got to the door, he was already back in his chair facing his computer.

Outside his office, I passed a pod of 12 or so producers all seemingly in their 30s silently tapping away at their computers, a window into my destiny. No newsroom laughter, no chatter, no bustle. It was a cemetery. His right-hand woman Arlene, old enough to be my aunt, escorted me along the planks of flooring to the elevator.

I can't ever resist asking someone about how he or she eventually landed at certain junctures in their life, so I asked Arlene about her path before CNN.

Her answer explained her battleship toughness, "I worked in the office of the Mayor of New York City."

"No doubt that prepped you for the wild and wooly world of CNN," I said.

"Oh yeah," she said, then hit the down arrow at the elevator bank. Before the doors shut between us, she added, "Working for Lou is not for everyone. I've seen a lot of people come and go. He's definitely an acquired taste."

She kindly stated what I already knew in my gut. I remain grateful.

Back at the office, my bosses and colleagues congratulated me. Yet, I knew something that they did not. This was not going to be pleasant. Sure, I landed the bigger salary, the bigger title, and the prestige of working with a big celebrity talent.

But then, I had to show up and go to work.

Getting it going

Anyone who has ever launched a news/talk show in the modern political era knows the birthing process - identify the position (left-right/Democrat-Republican-Independent), design a clock (where to insert commercials and time out the breaks), organize the bumper music in and out of those breaks, post the job openings ("Wanted: one engineer and three experienced producers"), hire the staff, find an announcer, book guests for those initial days... and on and on it goes.

For weeks, we were "a rocket-in-the-planning" stage, not even face-up on the launch pad yet (not that I'm comparing this to rocket science). Everyone knows it's just a matter of time before there's a first major shake-up. It's inevitable on every show. Meteors a-flying. The tension that builds before take-off eventually settles into cruise-mode. Or you hope.

After two months, I got the rocket onto the launch pad.

Then four months after that, I quit.

But I'm now getting ahead of myself.

Chapter Nineteen

FEUDS, STRESS AND LESSONS LEARNED

On-air brawls make for great talk show theater. Race Relations! Illegal Immigration! Abortion! Gun Control! Health Care! Gay Marriage! Legalized Pot! Producers love when passion booms out of the speakers. However, what happens behind-the-scenes when battles erupt between the staff and host is another story altogether.

I knew from the moment I landed the job with Lou Dobbs, trouble was brewing. It would just be a matter of time before I quit (or got fired).

The conflict inside my head

To be fair, Dobbs was honest with me from the very start during the job interview a few weeks earlier. The tipoff, of course, came with his exact words, "I'm a bastard," spoken at the start of our first face-to-face meeting.

Unfortunately, that was likely the first and last time we agreed on anything. If I had gone with my gut, I would have passed on the job. Instead, I surrendered to the new title "executive producer" and, of course, the 25 percent salary bump. In exchange, I played the part - smiling as I stood aside him at various functions announcing the show. Looking back, I was only victimized by my own miscalculation of how much I could tolerate what actually came with the job.

"Obviously, you're a fraud," my voice of reason whispered to a photo of smiley-faced me, standing next to the man from central casting with the mega-watt smile and monogrammed shirt cuffs. We had been photographed at a national convention with influential station managers (potential affiliates) and radio industry movers and shakers from around the country. Instead of feeling charged, I felt hollow.

I sold out and I knew it. I just didn't like the guy. On the surface, we saw eye to eye on certain political principles, yet we were light years apart on the spirit with which they should be executed.

What separates a talk show host from other commentators?

When Dobbs insisted on hiring a scriptwriter, I was struck silent. He actually wanted someone who would literally write out his monologues, transitions, and even interview segments with suggested questions and factoids.

A scriptwriter - for a talk show?

Spontaneity is the very essence of talk radio. It is the very heart of its beauty. If you script a talk show, you lose the genre. It becomes something... else.

Since when is a talk show scripted?

A talk show should not be scripted any more than play-by-play commentary of a sporting event. Imagine listening to the radio at the moment of the game-winning home run on October 3, 1951 when the normally calm-voiced Russ Hodges described the "shot heard round the world."

"There's a long drive... it's going to be, I believe... THE GIANTS WIN THE PENNANT!! THE GIANTS WIN THE PENNANT!! THE GIANTS WIN THE PENNANT!! THE GIANTS WIN THE PENNANT!!

"Bobby Thomson hits [it] into the lower deck of the left-field stands! The Giants win the pennant and they're goin' crazy, they're goin' crazy! HEEY-OH!!!"

Ten seconds followed with goose bump-raising crowd noise.

Hodges returned to the mic and exclaimed, *"I don't believe it! I don't believe it! I do not believe it! Bobby Thomson... hit a line drive... into the lower deck... of the left-field stands... and this place is goin' crazy! The Giants! Horace Stoneham has got a winner! The Giants won it... by a score of 5 to 4... and they're pickin' Bobby Thomson up... and carryin' him off the field!"*

You can't script that stuff. It's organic. Radio, the naked human voice, is the great exposer. You can't act your way into these thrills and revelry. It builds from within, goes deeper than words. It brings out the things that make us human. You can't read your way through the thrill of a winning home run, you must feel your way. Or there's a disconnect. The same principle applies in talk radio for the natural flow of conversation.

While everyone - managers, producers, and radio rats alike - agreed on this matter, no one wanted to be the one to tell Dobbs. Admittedly, we were all in the business of communication, yet none of us was willing to do so. The feud was doused before it ever actually ignited.

We hired four producers, an engineer, and yes, *a scriptwriter.*

The celebratory launch lunch

Seated around a 25-foot table inside the conference room were four owners of the company that I had now worked for over six years. Huddled together along one side was the newly appointed staff of producers, writer, and engineer whose resumes featured Ivy League schools and stints at ABC, CNN, and Fox television. On the other side were Dobbs, his publicist, his multi-functional associate, and a guy whose job had no title, (but was glued to his side at all times). The only thing missing was the marching band.

"Congratulations to our fine host," began USRN chairman and CEO, Nick Verbitsky. Smiles circled the table. "We're about to embark on extraordinary radio history."

The event was popping, the conversation was jazzed, and a positive charge filled the air. We producers were swapping ideas for show segments. Anti-free trade! Anti-globalization!

Then Lou Dobbs exploded.

"Who the fuck do you think you are?" he shouted across the table at a producer we'll call "Sam." "Haven't you read any of my books?"

All eyes darted to Sam. I could swear, the traffic on the street below stopped.

"Well no... I haven't," Sam stammered. Oy! All eyes shifted back to Dobbs as he leaned forward and, in a Darth Vader moment, snarled, "Then why the fuck are you sitting here?"

Foolishly, Sam continued to hype his segment idea, the very one that got him into this spot - an eclectic human interest story that fell beyond the tight boundaries of Dobbs' pet topics. Smart? No. But reason for verbal hand-grenades? Hardly.

Sam never learned Rule Number One. A talk show host is always right - even when he's wrong.

If only I charged for the door then. If only my feet were smarter than my seat. My voice of reason - the producer in my head - was yelling, *Get up and leave. Do it!*

But no, I was frozen. So was everyone else, as evidenced by the sandwiches and side dishes left untouched in the center of the table. As one witness aptly described it, "It was a fire-breathing moment." And she was seated outside the room about five cubicles away.

Afterwards, another colleague, who also heard the screaming match from her desk outside the conference room, asked, "Do you think it was because of Sam's ethnicity?" She happened to share Sam's Indian ethnicity, but not his Muslim religion.

"I do not," I answered. "I believe he's an equal opportunity hater." When I later told my husband about the incident, he responded, "No, Dobbs is *not a hater* - he's just an angry asshole."

Trying to survive

Deep down inside I knew that we - the producers - were part of the problem. Dobbs was intimidating and surly, all right, which when paired with his intelligent take on the economy, for example, gave the impression he was a superhero fighting the "bad banker guys." He had no fear, taking on Congress, the banks, and even the President of the United States. At least this was my perspective.

We also knew we were not paid to be entertained or loved by him. We were hired to support and protect his "brand." In other words - Rule Number Two: Support your host at all times. However, I had never experienced his "brand" of support staff treatment. And as you know by now, I had been around the block a few times in working closely with big time quirky personalities with unrestrained egos.

Even those of us with experience could create a false womb and put up with behavior we'd never even accept from our own mothers. Technically, we were enablers.

Sam was a talented producer with a culturally diverse schmooze-factor. Between his British accent and over-the-phone charm, he could wrangle in almost any hesitant guest. He would convince guests to come in studio LIVE, if only for a mere 10 minutes, during the middle of the day when the traffic through Times Square was most insane... not an easy task.

If only Dobbs appreciated this. Day after day, Sam was a target of Mr. Nasty's increasing wrath. Then one evening while the producers and engineer were decompressing in the control room after the show, a new fracas erupted along the order of the infamous conference room brawl.

Sam had nonchalantly said how much he disliked a particular caller during the "open phone" segment. It was as if he called Dobbs' mother a nasty name.

"Who the fuck do you think you are?" our boss shouted. So much for our post-production review of what worked or failed during the three-hour show.

The program had been broadcasting for a mere four weeks and we were becoming more and more familiar with his weird outbursts. However, that didn't necessarily make them easy to take.

"It's just his opinion," I yelled in the direction of my shoes, unable to look directly at yet another beating inflicted upon my co-worker. My effort to detonate the bomb was unsuccessful. They locked horns.

"What are you really asking me?" Sam asked, taking him on.

"You think you are so smart, don't you?" Dobbs shot back.

"Do you talk to me this way because I'm Muslim?"

The hum of the electronics filled the silence of the room. No one dared to breathe.

Then Dobbs said, "Why don't you and I step into the studio where we can continue this conversation?"

The rest of us - including the engineer - were relieved to stay behind in the control room, our hearts pounding. It was as painful as watching a parent lacerate a child over spilt milk. Then one producer broke the silence, "One good reason Sam's on staff? A stooge like him ensures that I keep my job longer than I expect. He's a great distraction."

Well maybe for *that* producer.

From our side of the glass, we watched the body language in the studio - intense but civil. They sat opposite one another, the console between them, their eyes fixed on one another, as if they were renegotiating their separate country's border lines.

Three days later the engineer on the show unexpectedly resigned. His final words to me, "This sucks. Radio is supposed to be fun."

Off he went into the sunrise of a new job. I was jealous.

Then came my turn

Despite the incident in the studio a few days earlier, nothing changed between Dobbs and Sam. My fellow producer continued to pour his heart into the job and Dobbs simmered and seethed. About a week after the scene in the control room, Dobbs called me at my desk early one morning from his car.

"Transfer this call back to a studio where no one can hear you," he commanded.

I'm not getting paid enough to do this.

After I picked up in the soundproof room, Dobbs immediately informed me, "You had better listen to what I'm saying - if one of us is going to be a horse's ass, it's going to be you." *What is THAT supposed to mean?*

I said nothing.

"It's time for you to fire Sam. He's done, do you hear me?"

Sam, at this point, was proving to be the most skillful among us. He expanded his contact list and tracked down guests that none of us ever thought could be gotten. Sam was golden.

"I can't fire him. We won't be able to replace him," I replied.

CLUNK! Dobbs hung up.

According to the blog of a former employee who described his own experience with Dobbs, "People were right to be afraid of him... Don't get me wrong - he could be fun and very charming. But his overall management style was built on intimidation. And I don't think that kind of leadership works. People simply don't make the best choices when they're nervous or scared."

The standoff with Geraldo

Of all the guests who came into the studio, talk show host and attorney Geraldo Rivera stirred up the most heat. But then again, why be surprised? He and Dobbs had a history. Geraldo was a pretty confident guy, given the accolades he accumulated as an investigative reporter with national celebrity status. Back in 1972, he exposed the real-life nightmares unfolding at a scandal-ridden New Jersey mental institution, Willowbrook State School. By doing so, he opened the door for a historic reform of mental disability care. This also put Geraldo's name on the map in journalism. It is, however, subject to interpretation and opinion whether he used that to build an admirably successful media career or squandered his stellar reputation by participating in stunts-gone-awry and less-than-classy on-air projects.

Fast forward to March 2009 when Geraldo is on a book tour with *His Panic: Why Americans Fear Hispanics in the U.S.* (Celebra Hardcover, 2008). Anyone watching TV or listening to talk radio regularly heard Geraldo take on Dobbs with issues of immigration. Of course, never with Dobbs in the same studio.

Here's a sample riff by Geraldo in reference to Dobbs: "He's almost singlehandedly responsible for creating, for being the architect of the young-Latino-as-scapegoat for everything that ails this country."

For days, we were anticipating the big showdown with Geraldo. And this was our first week. I had my own challenges with Dobbs, but I found myself protecting him as Geraldo sauntered into the green room with a camera crew, each over six feet tall. For the dramatic outcome, please refer back to the beginning of chapter 1.

A big lesson I learned that day - Dobbs' feuds became *my* feuds. This situation did not suit my nature.

Interestingly, he never mentioned one word about being married to a Hispanic woman nor that her parents were living on their property as well.

Dobbs was obviously more complicated than I expected. Certainly more principled. But principles are not always enough.

What's my part in all this?

We producers navigated the storms, finding our rhythm those first few weeks, grinding through dozens of morning papers and internet postings, zeroing in on show topics to present at the daily editorial meeting, targeting newsmakers and experts to spar with the host… and all the while, getting pepper-sprayed by our host with names such as "idiot," "sick-o," "moronic," and "bullshit-for-brains."

Even though USRN management knew what was going on behind-the-scenes, they literally chose to close their doors to it. Then one fateful day, one of the managers landed in the line of fire after making a show suggestion.

"You think you are so smart, don't you?" Mr. Nasty snarled at him in front of the entire sales department, adding a few F-bombs just to land his point in the way he knew best. That manager whimpered away and we came to see that no one was immune.

Those of us who worked in studio were at the epicenter, an epicenter that was morphing into a most bizarre shrine. It contained a poster-sized cover of Dobbs on *TALKERS* magazine, a variety of framed enlarged prints of his books, and best of all… a life-sized cardboard cutout of him standing in his navy power suit and red tie, looking very presidential.

One of the funniest experiences I had during that time happened on the same day I got into my feud with Dobbs over firing Sam. Upon reporting the run-in with my USRN bosses, one of the sales guys marched "Cardboard Lou" into the meeting, just for illustration purposes. We nearly fell off our chairs. I guess you had to be there.

As one former staffer observed about his temporary job on Dobbs' television show, "Get used to it if you wish to survive. You don't necessarily see this yet, but his manner is designed to build loyalty. *It's all a test.*"

Maybe he was right. The problem, however, was that I felt more like a hostage than an employee. There was one nagging question I could not ignore. If I stayed (meaning survived) on this job, wouldn't I become part of the problem?

Another day, another drama

About seven weeks after the launch of the show (and three months into my contract), the staff was sitting in our daily editorial meeting at that same conference table now memorialized by our infamous celebratory lunch. As usual, Dobbs connected from his home through the speakerphone. For the first 10 minutes, we discussed the day's lineup, potential guests, and the debates at hand. A storm of fire trucks blasted along the street below. As luck would have it, they remained stuck in traffic for at least 10 minutes, totally drowning out the conversation. For the producers, it was just another day in Midtown-Manhattan. We learned to pause until after they passed.

"Young lady," Dobbs bellowed, loud enough for me to hear through the speaker. (And being the only female, I knew whom he was addressing). "How dare you call me when sirens are sounding." And then, clunk, he hung up.

I wanted to shout to the firemen below, "Quick - there's a talk show host on fire up here." In fact, for the rest of the day, Dobbs ignored my efforts to reconnect by phone so we could finish the conversation. I hoped he liked the lineup.

This was getting old very quickly.

We gotta get outta this place

"How about my old job back?" I begged my former manager for the third time in 10 days.

"Give it time. The launch of a show can be challenging," he fired back.

"I've given it time. This is a bad fit."

"Let's talk. Just not today," he said, shooing me from his office.

I returned 24 hours later, standing by the door and asking, "Is today a good day?"

"Some other time," he said, never even looking up from his "crackberry."

The next day, I returned with a list of conflicts and concerns with the show - the crazy feuds that were unfolding - and warned this same manager that I smelled a lawsuit brewing (though I assured him it wasn't from me).

"Perhaps it's time for a meeting," he said. And a day later, about six of us sat around the table on a conference call with Lou's attorney-manager.

How many of these conversations has this attorney had over the years? I wondered.

The meeting lasted 15 minutes and like a human ping-pong ball, I was back at my desk. If the dynamics changed, I hadn't noticed.

The job of keeping a job - while quitting

By the seventh week of the battle, the producer inside my head whispered, *"Of course, you could always quit..."*

True.

"Don't!" My greatest advisor and best friend advised. "Not necessary - and not in this economy. Instead, tell management that you wish to be 'repositioned.'"

Repositioned? *Repositioned?*

Which was exactly what I asked - or respectfully *demanded* - the next morning. I practiced the words over and over and over until they were my own.

Management never asked why. They knew. As quickly as I was hired onto the show, I was ushered off. My new desk was set in the low-rent district between the copy machine and bathroom. For the next month, I was on "temporary reassignment." Not that anyone (including me) knew what it was. My new motto became, look busy - they can't hit a moving target!

My salary was cut by $20,000 from when I was originally hired. I felt like I was in a witness protection program, searching for my new identity. But I still had a job.

Rocky aftermath

Dobbs handpicked the replacement executive producer, whose first job was to do the thing I never would - fire Sam. But Sam did not leave quietly. He filed a lawsuit, which the company settled out-of-court. I knew this to be true because I was called into the HR office to listen to seven pages or so of the document describing several of the now infamous conflicts described in this chapter. I verified them all.

Six months later, the executive producer who replaced me resigned, stating he wanted to "spend more time with his family." *His* replacement lasted two years, followed by another who was fired after three weeks. The next (and last) EP survived 18 months, when the show finally fizzled out and went off the air with little fanfare or industry attention.

So, what's a producer to learn?

In Rosie O'Donnell's best-seller at the time, *Celebrity Detox* (Grand Central Publishing, 2007), she cast light on the pitfalls of her own fame, blaming the steady stream of praise showered onto celebrities as a destructive syndrome. She struck a chord with this excerpt:

"It's a shift that happens in the head and that very few celebrities will ever really speak about - the inflation of self, the pride. One begins to believe in the specialness and a dangerous sense of entitlement takes over. It feels shameful to speak of, and I do not do it easily. The drunkenness is not from alcohol or morphine; it's from the steady stream of praise pouring in.

"Let me put it this way: Life is full of red lights and stop signs. When celebrity addiction starts, you become impatient with, even angry at those necessary obstacles. You think you can run a red light or two... And then you do."

I'm resigned to never knowing the whole truth when it came to the crazy happenings working on that show. However, like a bee sting, it hurt at the time... but now it's just an interesting story.

Epilogue

Many colleagues from my early days in the business have moved on to new fields. Perhaps, some have found more engaging purposes in their lives since we first landed in the talk biz together. One launched her own PR firm that specializes in computer company upstarts. Another got his degree as a psychologist and hung out a shingle. Still another became a lawyer. The guy I least expected to leave the sacred altar of talk shows became a banker. *A banker?*

Three of the hangers-on climbed up the radio managerial ladder. I hope they're happy.

But then again, who am I to judge others? I left as well. In the talk show game - especially these days - it's move on or stagnate... or worse, be tossed to the sidewalk.

Hanging up the headphones

Because talk show producers don't traditionally have a voice in front of the mic, I'm grateful to have the opportunity to express myself here. We provide support for the biggest blabbermouths in broadcasting history and while we don't always agree with them, our job is to keep shoveling the coal so they can do what they do, hour after hour, show after show.

After more than three decades of working among some of the better-known in this business, I finally hung up my headphones. Terrorist attacks, anti-abortion bombs, the O.J. Simpson murder trial, the Scott Peterson case, the Oklahoma bombing, the Columbine High School shootings - these were just some stories I trudged through with my gunky-muddy-work-boots, sometimes for months at a time. On most days, after hours of plodding through evil, revenge, outrage and righteous indignation, all spinning out of control, I'd get those boots home, but never completely cleaned off.

I've heard that "happy" news exists in the world too - but who talks about that? What's there to debate? Let's face it, in countries where most of the news in the media is positive - they are almost always totalitarian regimes. Freedom of speech and freedom of the press - as well as responsible journalism - are not tidy processes.

Recently on NPR, a war correspondent I had once booked said she was ready to leave the frontlines of war and return to a quieter setting. Like a *newsroom*. I guess it's all relative. Her reasoning, she said, was a syndrome called "compassion fatigue." She may not have been pulling a trigger or aiming an explosive, but she was clearly absorbing the distress.

In retrospect, the two concerns that have bothered me most about this career are ones I may never quite be able to understand.

First, the work was too often about the fight for its own sake, sometimes for the sole purpose to grab attention (translation, *ratings*). Is demonizing the "dangers" of a competing political ideology really more important than focusing on an oil spill that's causing horrifying ecological damage?

Second, there's always a so-called "expert" out there anxious to take any, and I mean ANY, position on a topic - even at the cost of their personal *truth* - in order to get their name, face, or voice on the air. What we often see and hear is the process of trading the "truth" for the sake of promoting a brand or ego. I worry that we are far more focused on attaining victory than truth on all levels of our society today - and *that*, in my opinion, is a dangerous form of creeping corruption.

Big changes

Of course, I experienced other changes, too. I got married. For the first time - and at the age of 50. The delay, of course, as anyone who knows me well can attest, was simply because I just couldn't decide on the silverware pattern. Well, okay, not exactly.

While I know I do not really need to explain myself here, I will anyway. As a kid growing up in Queens with an immigrant mother, I instinctively grasped there was a bigger world calling for me to explore. As Pinterest puts it, "Places to go, People to meet, Things to do... Life to be lived!" Corny? Perhaps. But that was me.

Thanks to being in this business, I travelled the world, met some of the most interesting people, viewed the passing parade of current events, and gathered stories along the way. The talk show producer business afforded me many gifts.

However, with the passing of time and a set of crow's feet emerging at the corners of my eyes, I've come to realize that the very place where I am today is exactly where I need to be and certainly where I *should* be. This is not something that I might have understood at 25. (Or even 30, 35, or 40.)

Many college friends, who went on to get married, have children, and lead more traditional lives, viewed my early choices as boxed-in. Literally. After all, I was living in a 9 x 12 foot studio apartment on the Upper West Side of Manhattan for 20 years. When I wasn't working in windowless studios, I usually operated within the cramped confines of three panel barriers without a ceiling in a corporate cubicle farm. And the salary of a radio producer - even one based in New York City - is, with few exceptions, in the realm of an underpaid teacher. Yet for me, my choice was an ever-expanding universe, given the prestigious companies I had the privilege to work for and the headline-worthy people I regularly met.

Shortly after getting married, I left my sliver of Manhattan and moved to New England where more woods and rivers surround me than sidewalks. I've actually heard a tree falling in the forest. For the first time ever, I witnessed eagles soar overhead and land in my backyard. My life has taken a gentler turn - but certainly not a less active one.

Not that the transition was easy. After all, I was convinced that when I left New York and my role in the trenches as a talk show producer, I had also left behind my "life." And guess what? I did.

However, the last eight years have shown me that I traded it in for something deeper, or really deeper inside myself. And I'm talking about both personally *and* professionally.

Another opening, another show

I married a man named Michael Harrison whose career and business is right in the thick of today's multimedia scene. He is the publisher of two leading radio industry trade journals – *TALKERS* for talk radio (www.talkers.com) and *RadioInfo* for music radio (www.radioinfo.com). He is also a radio show creator, convention organizer, corporate consultant, management advisor, and talent coach - not to mention one of news media's leading "go-to" guys when insight into a breaking story about radio and its related fields is needed. He's regularly called to be in front of the radio mics and TV cameras as an analyst on a daily basis and he is widely regarded as a leading media theorist.

In the basement of our rustic, New England home, a professional grade radio studio takes up about the same space as my old apartment. It operates as the brain center of his broadcasting activities, which include the development of experimental shows and numerous on-air and online activities. I've gotten into the habit of keeping my cell phone ringer turned off because it seems the whole house is "on the air."

The cable networks regularly invite him to appear as a talking head live via link-up through local TV stations or Skype to explain the latest talk show controversy or the political implications of the media's impact on any given issue. And when no link is available or Skype won't suffice, camera crews show up in our living room - such as recent visits by CNN and MSNBC. Michael might launch into a diatribe about Freedom of Speech or "the impact of talk radio on elections," or even "the way the internet is rewiring the human nervous system." The topics are endless.

Among the many skills I've honed in this marriage? I've learned to roll with whatever happens next - an invitation to the White House Correspondents Dinner, a brainstorm session with a United States Senator or an up-and-coming talent about the proper skill-set for buffing up a talk show, or even, "Hey, why don't you write a book about your amazing career as a talk show producer?" My husband lives an intense, unpredictable sort of life, which is an exciting continuation of the road I was already traveling alone. All of which leads me right back to the same old question, *Hey - how did I get here? Me? A girl from Queens.*

What's the best part about being married to someone so engaged in the radio business - a man who is both an intensely serious intellect, and a zany, devil-may-care clown? Ah! That's where the *personal* side of my life has become even richer and more rewarding than I could ever have imagined.

My husband, best friend, and business partner is fun, high-spirited, and most important, loving. He also makes me laugh every single day.

While this new life taps into my experiences of the past, I recognize that I am standing on the brink of something new.

So for me, the experiences and observations shared in this book served as preparation for the adventures that await me in this exciting new chapter of my life.

Bernadette and Rush Limbaugh in 2013 at the NAB Radio Show in Orlando.

Almost too close for comfort: **Bernadette and Bill Cosby in 1991 during comedian's visit to the Larry King Show. Cosby thought it would be "interesting" if he posed behind Bernadette looking sideways. Strange.**

Bernadette and then-boss Lou Dobbs in 2008 at the *Radio & Records* Convention in Washington, DC.

Bernadette with then-boss Tom Snyder in 1995.

Bernadette and then-boss Dick Oliver in 1990 in his cluttered *New York Daily News* office.

Bernadette stopping by to visit her old CBS Radio colleague Charles Osgood circa 2000.

Promotional sheet for "The Bulldog Edition" moving from WOR to WEVD in 1993.

Index

A

ABC, xii, 18
 News Radio, 120, 134
 Radio Networks, 52, 83, 101, 142, 190, 211
 television, 90, 105
Advocacy journalism, 195-96
Ahmadinejad, Iranian President Mahmoud, 154
Aiello, Danny, 58
Ailes, Roger, 21
Albright, Madeleine, 154-56
Alexander, Jason Allen, 167
Alexander, Julie, 66, 68
Altria (publisher), 21
AM band, 16
Amazon, 21
"America's Talking," 83
America's Voices in Israel, 168
"American Idol," 156, 157
"Anderson Cooper 360," 139
Anderson, Kurt, 196
Anderson, Loni, 127, 129
Anka, Paul, 67
"Arsenio Hall Show, The," 179
Ashcroft, John, 3, 152–53
Associated Press, (AP), 10, 47
TheAtlantic.com, 199
Attorney General of the United States, 3, 152, 153
Auntie Mame, 54
Aviv, Juval, 135-36

B

Baba-Booey, 40
Back to the Batcave, 105
Bantam Books, 176
Baradt, David, 173
Barnes & Noble, 5
Barondess, Mark, 68
Barrymore, Drew, 90
Bartlett, Dave, 30
"Batman," (TV show), 77
 and Catwoman, 105
 and Robin, 12
 movie with Michael Keaton, 104
 on ABC-TV, 105
 starring Adam West, 105
Beatles, 26
Beck, Glenn, 5, 29, 117, 118, 178
 The Blaze, 118
Begala, Paul, 149-50
Behar, Joy, 4, 112-13
Bell, Catherine, 102, 105
 as Sarah Mackenzie, 102
Benny, Jack, 44
Bensman, Todd, 204
Bergen, Peter, 135
Berkley Trade, 105
Bernstein, David, 164
Bias: A CBS Insider Exposes How the Media Distort the News, 203
Biddles Barrow, Mayflower Madame Sidney, 20
Biden, Joe, 186-89

Big Apple, xiii, 8, 48, 56, 126, 132
Black, Lewis, 3, 151-52
Blaze, The, 118
"Blind Side, The," 148
Bobbitt, Lorena, 88
John, 88
Bohannon, Jim, 29
Bonaduce, Danny, 166-67
"Breaking Bonaduce," 166
"The Next Mrs. Bonaduce," 167
Bono, Sonny, 181
Brady, James, 178
"Brady Bunch, The," 167
Branch Davidian religious sect, 74
Brando, Marlon, 69
"Breaking Bonaduce," 166
Brokaw, Tom, 58
Bubba the Love Sponge, 86
Buckley Jr., William F., 67
"Bulldog Edition," definition of, 8 (also see *New York Daily News*)
Bullock, Sandra, 147-49
"Burden of Proof," 89
Burns and Allen, 44
Bush, George H. W., 22, 180
Bush, George W., 19, 22, 127, 149, 181, 182
Business Plus, (publisher), 202
Buttafuoco, Joey, 89-90
wife, Mary Jo, 90

C

Capese, Jerry, 9
Capitol Hill, 142
Capitol Offense, 179
"Car Talk," 32
Carey, Drew, 107-08
book, *Dirty Jokes and Beer: Stories of the Unrefined*, 107
Carlin, George, 4
Carson, Johnny, 101, 144
Carson, Kit, 27
Carter, Bill, 106
Carter, Jimmy, 59, 172, 176-78, 181
book, *Keeping Faith*, 176
Carter, Lynda, 67
Carville, James, 109
CBS, xii, 4, 14, 34, 76, 77, 79, 80, 82, 84, 93, 94, 96, 97, 112, 113, 134,142, 203
Broadcast Center, 79, 81, 93, 94, 96
"Evening News," 23, 78, 83
Radio Mystery Theater, 81
Radio Network, 69, 115
"Sunday Morning," 93
Talk Radio, xii, 14, 99
television, 100, 101, 115, 124,145, 203
Television City, 80
Celebra (publishing), 216
"Celebrity Apprentice," 157
Celebrity Detox, 222
"Celebrity Rehab with Dr. Drew," 91
Center Street (publishing), 152, 190
Chafets, Zev, 21
Cheney, Dick, 19
Cher, 180-81
Chung, Connie, 79-80
Clapton, Eric, 36
Clark, Prosecutor Marcia, 89
Clinton, Bill, 19, 22, 83, 149, 157, 165, 176, 179
Clinton, Hillary, 186
Clooney, George, 142, 165, 183-85

CNN,
(also, Cable News Network), 1, 23, 56, 70, 71, 83, 89, 127, 135, 139, 149, 181, 194, 195, 196, 198, 199, 206, 211, 227
CNN.com, 23
Colford, Paul, 84
Colmes, Alan, xi, 139
Color codes, 134-36
Columbine High School, 224
commie-pinko libs, 19
Condit, Gary, 127
Cooper, Alice, 74
Cooper, Anderson, 137, 139, "Anderson Cooper 360," 139
Cosby, Bill, 58, (photo) 229
Costas, Bob, 59-60
Cronkite, Walter, 113
"Crossfire," 59, 149
Cruise, Tom, 167
Cunningham, Billy, 67
Cuomo, Governor Mario, 67

D

Daily News, (see *New York Daily News*)
Daily Planet, 10
"Dan Rather Reporting," 82
Darth Vader, 211
Davis, Geena, 58
Dear Abby, 37, 50
Delacourt (publishing), 21
Delaware, 134
Dell (books), 68
Dell'Abate, Gary, 40, 128-30
Deputy President Pro Tempore, 58
Dershowitz, Alan, 172
Dickinson, Angie, 71
Discovery Channel, 147
Disney, Walt, 72
Dobbs, Lou, xi, 1, 7, 181-221, (photo) 229
Donahue, Phil, 191
Downey Jr., Morton, 18, 118
Dr. Ruth, 165
Dr. Seuss, animated film "Horton Hears a Who!," 99
Dreyfuss, Richard, "Mr. Holland's Opus," 111
Drudgereport.com, 23
Dunkin' Donuts, 2

E

E! Television, 3, 163
"Ed Sullivan Show," 7
Edwards, John, 3
EFM Media Management, 18
Elvis, 26
Emmy (award), 37, 54
Empire State Building, 132-33
"Entertainment Tonight," 89
environmental wackos, 19
Executive Office Building, 176
Exporting America, 202
"Eye to Eye with Connie Chung," 79

F

"Family Affair," 115
Fantasia, 156-57
(also, Fantasia Barrino)
"Fashion Police," 3, 164
Federal Communications Commission, (FCC), 34, 84, 86
Femi-Nazis, 19
Ferguson, Colin, 76
Fifth Avenue, 9, 24, 77
Fisher, Amy, 89-91
adult film,"Amy Fisher: Totally Nude & Exposed," 90
book, *If I Knew Then*, 90

on "Celebrity Rehab with Dr. Drew," 91
on truTV's "The Smoking Gun Presents," 90
Florida Atlantic University, 70
Fluke, Sandra, 16, 17, 23
Ford, Gerald, 178
Forest, Elliott, 100
Forman, Arlene, 199, 206
Forty-Eight Hours (48 Hours), 77, 80, 96
Fox, Michael J., 182-83
Fox News, xii, 21, 83, 89, 139, 142, 189, 190, 211
Franken, Al, 21
Free Press, 59
Freud, Sigmund, 51

G

Gallagher, Mike, xi, 132-33
Gallo, Bill, 10
Gallo, Hank, 9
Gangland, 9
Gawker.com, 200
Gettinger, Ruby, 156-57
Giants, 210
"Gimme My Reality Show," 89
Gladstone, Brooke, xiii
Godfrey, Arthur, 44, 46
Goldberg, Bernie, 203
Goldberger, Myrna, 70
Golden, James, 24-25
"Good Day New York," 13
"Good Morning America," 78, 83
Gore, Al, 82, 157, 181, 191
Grand Central Publishing, 222
Grant, Lou, 8, 13, 65, 203
Gross, Gil, 79-81, 83-84, 86, 90, 94, 95, 229
Grossman Publishing, 191

H

Haddad, Tammy, 69
Hannity, Sean, xi, 5, 135, 137, 139
"Hannity & Colmes," 139
Hansen (spy scandal), 152
Hansen, Eric, (see producers)
Harcourt, 63
"Hardball," 5
Harding, Tonya, 82
Harper (publishing), 154, 162
Harrison, Michael, 26, 226-28
Hartmann, Thom, xi
Harvey, Paul, 83
Helmsley, Sherman, 101
Herzog, President of Israel, Chaim, 171
His Panic: Why Americans Fear Hispanics in the U.S., 216
Hodges, Russ, 209-10
Holloway, Dave, 88
daughter, Natalee, 88
Hollywood, 104, 115, 121, 122, 123, 138, 147, 166, 167, 179
and Hollywood-ization, 179
Holmes, Katie, 167
Homeland Security, Department of, 134, 135
Hope, Bob, 44
"House Guest," 89
Huckabee, Governor Mike, 179, 189-90
Huffington, Arianna, 165
(The) Hulk, 199, 205
Hulu.com, 71
Hussein, Saddam, 155

Hyperion (publishing), 166

I

"Imus in the Morning," 186
Independents Day: Awakening the American Spirit, 201
Inside-the-Beltway, 59
Is Our Children Learning: The Case Against George W. Bush," 149
ISDN, a digital phone line, 82, 98, 141, 196
Israel, 168-74
Israeli Defense Force, (IDF), 172
iUniverse (publishing), 90

J

Jackson, Michael, 88
Jackson, Reverend Jesse, 82
"JAG," 102, 105
James, Jesse, 147-49
  West Coast Choppers, 147
"Jaws," 111
"Jeffersons, The," 101
"Jerry Springer Show, The,"146-47
Jerusalem Post, The, 174
"Jesse James is a Dead Man," 148
Jihadist, 137, 138, 204
Jimmy the engineer, 44, 46
"Judge Judy," 121
"Judge Mills Lane," 121

K

KABC-TV, (Los Angeles), 74, 101
Kaelin, Kato, 89
Kardashian, Bob, 89
  "Keeping Up with the Kardashians," 89
Keaton, Michael, 105
Keeping Faith, 176
Kennedy, Jack, 9, 119, 177
Kerry, John, 181, 182, 184, 185
KFBK, (Sacramento), 18, 118
Kilborn, Craig, 116
King, Larry, xi, 2, 4, 7, 15, 19, 32, 56-73, 118, 119, 137, 229
  CableACE Awards, 63
  King of Late Night Radio, 62
  King of Talk, 57
  "Larry King Live," 56
  Peabody Awards, 63
  Sultan of Smooch, 69
  books,
  Mr. King, You're Having a Heart Attack, 68
  My Remarkable Journey, 70, 119
  On the Line: The New Road to the White House, 63
  play about, *The Many Wives of Larry King*, 70
Kirkpatrick, Jeanne, 20
Klein, Dennis, 101
KMED (Medford, Or), 158
Koppel, Ted, 101
Koresh, David, 74-78
KQV, (Pittsburgh), 118
Kreskin, 165
Kroft, Steve, 82
Kuralt, Charles, 93
KXAR, (Hope, Arkansas), 189

L

Lamott, Anne, 119
"Larry Sanders Show, The," 101
"Late Late Radio Show with Tom Snyder, The," 100, 113, 115
"Late Night with David Letterman," 101
"Later with Bob Costas," 60

Lehrer, Jim, 93
Leno, Jay, 189, 193
Letterman, Dave, 58, 100, 101, 144, 145-46, 189
Levin, Carl, (D-Mi), 203
Levin, Mark, xi
Levy, Chandra, 127
Life Is Not a Fairy Tale, 157
Limbaugh, Rush, xi, 5, 16-29, 32, 118, 176, 178, 180, 182, 183, (photo) 229
  books, *I Told You So*, 21
  The Way Things Ought to Be, 21
Lincoln Bedroom, 22, 180
Lionel Trains, 115-16
  videos:
  "A Century of Legendary Lionel Trains;" 115
  "Celebrity Train Layouts 2: Tom Snyder," 115
LK, (also see Larry King), 63, 65, 70
Long Island Lolita, 90
Long Island Press, 90
Lopez, Mario, 167

M

Mackenzie, Sarah, (see Catherine Bell)
MADtv, 89
Magliozzi, Tom and Ray, 32
Maher, Bill, 80
Mandela, Nelson, 65
Manigault-Stallworth, Omarosa, 157
Manson, Marilyn, 65
Marzulli, John, 9
Mason, Steve, 100
Matthews, Chris, 59, 137
McBride, Mary Margaret, 44
McCain, John, 4,
McDonald's, 30
McGrath, Bob, 114
  "Bob" from "Sesame Street"
McLaughlin, Ed, 18
McVeigh, Timothy, 152
Media exhibitionist, 69, 164-65
"Meet the Press," 59
Meigs, Jim, 205
Meyer, Bill, 158
Miami Herald, 118
Michelini, Alex, 9
Milch, David, 110
  "Deadwood," "John from Cincinnati," 110
Mitchell, George, 58
"Monster Garage," 147
Moore, Michael, 191
"Mr. Holland's Opus," 111
Mr. Ring-a-Ding-Ding, 103
MSNBC, 59, 227
Multimedia Television, 51
Murrow, Edward R., 82
Muslim, 134, 137, 138, 212, 214
My Remarkable Journey, (see Larry King)
Myers, Neil, 3, 38
  "Neil Myers Show, The," 56
Mystery Science Theater 3000, 129

N

N-Word-gate, 163
Nader, Ralph, 190-91
NASCAR, 102
National Association of Broadcasters Hall of Fame, 93
NBC, xii,
  NBC News, 78, 186
  NBC Radio Networks, 29, 37, 44, 47, 50, 51, 52, 53, 56, 69

NBC-TV, 60, 80, 101
Netanyahu, Benjamin, 172
Never Again: Securing America and Restoring Justice, 152
New Hampshire Primary, 4, 120
New Jersey Hirailers, 116
New Media Seminar, 25, 54
Freedom of Speech Award, 26-27
New *Yawkers*, 8
New York Daily News, 8, 14, 17, 24, 84
New York Magazine, 196
New York minute, 8
New York Post. 66, 68
New York Times, The, 21, 28, 68, 106, 127, 157, 166, 190
Newmar, Julie, 105 (Catwoman)
News Journal, The, 187
"Nightline," 101
Nixon, Richard, 63
Noonan, Peggy, 20
Norville, Deborah, 82
Nothing's Sacred, 151
Now, Let Me Tell You What I Really Think, 59
NPR, 161
Nude Picture-gate, 159

O

O'Brien, Conan, 72
O'Donnell, Rosie, 222
O'Neill. Tip, 59
Obama, Barack, 179, 188, 196
Oklahoma bombing, 224
Oliver, Dick, 8-15, (photo) 230
Omarosa, 157-59
"On the Media," xiii
"On the Record," 89
Opie and Anthony, 86
Original Brooklyn Water Bagel Company, (see Larry King), 70
Oscars, 180
Osgood, Charles, xi, 2, 7, 83, 93-99, (photo) 230
in animated film "Horton Hears a Who!," 99
Marconi Award, 93
"Osgood Files," 93
Peabody Award, 93
Radio Mercury Award, 93
OxyContin, 26

P

Page Six, 66, 67, 145, 147
Paley, William, 96
Palm Beach Post, 23
"Partridge Family, The," 166
"PBS NewsHour," 93
Pentagon, 135
People magazine, 9, 54, 58, 99
"The People's Court," 121
Perezhilton.com, 147
Perkins, Ma, 44
Peterson, Scott, 223
Phoners, definition of, 180, 183
Pinterest, 225
Piper, Pat, 69
Pocket Books, 21, 202
"The Point," 89
"Politically Incorrect," 80, 193
Politico.com, 23
Pope John Paul II, 83
Popular Mechanics, 205
POTUS, 176
Povich, Maury, 79
Powell, Colin, 127
Premiere, 142
Pretenders, 18

producer,
as career choice, 1-7
definition of, 5
Dell'Abate, Gary, 40, 128, 130
Golden, James, 24, 25
Hansen, Eric, 133
Pukehead, 156
Sam (pseudonym), 211-15, 218, 221
Pulitzer Prize, 9

Q

Quayle, Dan, 22
Quit Digging Your Grave with a Knife and Fork, 190
Quivers, Robin, 128-29

R

Radio terrorist, 40
RadioInfo.com, 227
Ramsey, JonBenet, 127
Random Acts of Badness, 166
Raphael, Sally Jessy, xi, 2, 7, 15, 30, 32, 35-55, 59, 85, 86, 229
children; adopted, biological, and foster:
J.J., 42
Allison, 42, 54
Andrea, 42
Catherine, 42
Darragh, 42
Dear Abby of the Airwaves, 37, 50
Sallyisms, 37-39, 40
book, *Sally: Unconventional Success*, 49
Rather, Dan, 58, 81-82, 83, 93
Read My Pins: Stories from a Diplomat's Jewel Box, 154
Reagan, Ronald, 20, 178
Regnery Publishing, 203
Reuters, 10, 78
Richards, Mary, 65
Rivera, Geraldo, 1, 2, 216-17
Rivers, Joan, 3, 163-64
Rob, (of Howard Stern show), 128-29
Roberts, John, 82
Rose, Pete, 86
Rossmiller, Shannen, 204-05
Rotten, Johnny, 110
RT America television, 71
Ruby's Diary: Reflections on All I've Lost and Gained," 156
Rush (as in Limbaugh), see Limbaugh
Rush Limbaugh: An Army of One, 21
Rush Limbaugh Is a Big Fat Idiot, 21
"Rush Limbaugh the TV Show," 21
"Rush to Excellence" tours, 21
"Rush & Molloy," (George and Joanna), 9
Dr. Ruth, 165

S

Salem Communications, 132
Sally: Unconventional Success, 36
Sallyisms, 37-39, 40
Salon.com, 23
Sam the Cabbie, 10
Samuels, Lynn, 20
The San Antonio Express-News, 204
San Francisco Examiner, 59
Sanders, Larry, 101-02
"Saturday Night Live," 106

"Saturday Night with Connie Chung," 80
"Saved by the Bell," 167
Schiavo, Michael, 91-92
  Terri, 91
  book,
  "*Terri: The Truth*" (Dutton, 2006), 91
Schlessinger, Dr. Laura, 159-63
School of Culinary Arts, 42
Scientology, 102
Secret Service, 177-78
Secretary of State, 154-56
Senate Majority Leader, 58
Sentinel HC, 21
September 11, 2001, (also, 9/11), 94, 126, 127, 130, 131, 134, 135, 136, 140, 152, 169, 172, 176, 177, 193
"Sesame Street," 114
Seventeen Magazine, 14, 61
Shakespeare, 54
Shandling, Garry, 101
Shankin, Paul, 19
Shatner, William, 82
Shavers, Cheryl, former Under Secretary for Technology at the Commerce Department, 157-58
Sheffield Farms Company, 96
Shields, Brooke, 82
Shoebat, Wallid, 137-40
Simmons, Gene, 82
Simon & Schuster, 63, 149
Simon Spotlight Entertainment, 151
Simpson, O. J., 3, 88-89, 92, 223
"60 Minutes," 77, 176
Slick, Grace, 36
Smith, Patti, 191
Smoking Gun, The, 23, 90
Snapple, 104
  Wendy the spokesperson, 104
Snapple-tini, 104
Snyder, Tom, 2, 7, 15, 100-17, (photo) 229
  as performed by Dan Aykroyd, 106
  Colortini, 104
  KABC-TV, (Los Angeles), 101
  "The Tomorrow Show," 101
  WABC-TV "Eyewitness News," 101
Soderlund, Karl, 42, 48, 49, 50
Southern Command, 24
Southwick, Shawn, 57, 70
Space: The Next Business Frontier, 202
Speaker of the House, 59
Spears, Britney, 167
  and marriage to Jason Allen Alexander
Spike TV, 148
Springer, Jerry, 146-47
  Mayor of Cincinnati, 147
St. Martin's Press, 49, 84
St. Patrick's Cathedral, 86
St. Patrick's Day Parade, 9
St. Tropez, France, 98
Stahl, Leslie, 82
Starbucks, 10, 11, 151
Starcasm.net, 71
Starship Enterprise, 29
Stern, Howard, 34, 40, 84, 127-31
  FCC fines, 84
  Howard Stern, King of All Media: The Unauthorized Biography, 84
  King of all Media, 84
  "The Howard Stern Show," 84, 90, 127-31
Stewart, Rod, 36

Stoneham, Horace, 210
Stop Whining and Start Living, 162
Studio 54, 10
studio flies, 41, 59
Style Network, 156
Super Bowl Prison Party, 3
Superman, 11, 12, 26
Sutton, Larry, 9

T

talk media, 22, 116, 192
talk radio sausage, xiii
Talkers, 19, 25, 26, 54, 69, 178, 218, 227
Los Angeles Regional Talkers Forum, 69
TALKNET, 38, 50
temporary reassignment, 221
Thatcher, Margaret, 83
Themal, Harry F. 187
Thompson, Rep. Bennie, (D-Mississippi), 135
Thomson, Bobby, 210
Tiger, 2
Time magazine, 64-65, 127
"Tomorrow Show, The," 101
"Tonight Show, The," 72, 101
Touchstone (publishing), 157
truTV, 90
Trump, Donald, 10, 157, 165
Tunick, Maurice, 52
Turner, Ted, 67
TV Guide, 104

U

"*Uh Oh! Gotta Go! Potty Tales from Toddlers*," 114
United Stations Radio Networks, (USRN), xii, 140, 142, 190, 195, 198, 202, 211, 218
United Theological Seminary, 158
Unsafe at Any Speed, 191
"Up to the Minute," 83

V

Van Susteren, Greta, 89
Verbitsky, Nick, 211
VH1 cable network, 166
Vietnam, 9, 152
"The View," 179
Viking (publisher), 194, 201, 202
Vilsack, Tom, 190
VoIP (Voice Over Internet Protocol), 141

W

WABC Radio (New York), 20
WABC-TV "Eyewitness News," 101
Wall Street Journal, The, 117
Walsh, Ed, 15
War of Words, 22
War on the Middle Class, 194, 201
Washington Monthly, 194
Washington Post, 23, 152
Way Things Ought To Be, The, 21
Weather Channel, 134
Webb, Jimmy, 110
"The Week in Review," 83
Weinstein Books, 70, 119
West, Adam, 105
(also, "Batman," ABC-TV show)
West Coast Choppers, 147
Whitcomb, Meg, 53
White House Correspondents' Dinner, 227
Whittaker, Johnny, 115
William Morrow, 156

Williams, Barry, 167
Williams, Brian, 186
Williams, Bruce, 19, 34
Williams, Ted, 72
Willowbrook State School, 216
Winfrey, Oprah, 118
Winkler, Henry, 165
WIOD-AM (Miami), 118
WMCA-AM, (New York), xii, 6, 36
WNYW-TV, (New York), 13
Wood, Fran, 17
WOR Radio (New York), xii, 8, 134, 176
World Trade Towers, 94, 128, 131, 132
(also World Trade Center)
WTVJ-TV's "Miami Undercover," 118

Y

Yahav, Yona, Mayor of Haifa, 173
Yapper, xi, 73
Yates, Andrea, 127
YouTube, 69, 110, 115, 182

Z

Zeiger, Lawrence Harvey, (see Larry King), 57

Acknowledgments

Producing a talk show comes with multiple challenges – and now I've learned, so does writing a book about such a career choice. With that in mind, I thank the many people who offered their time and talents to refine this project.

My husband Michael Harrison, for believing in me, his editor's eye, and the many layers he brought to the project.

The talk show hosts who recognized my enthusiasm, hired me, then actually became a part of the stories that landed between the covers. If it wasn't for Oliver, Sally, Larry, Gil, Charlie, Tom and yes, Lou, I would not have been able to write this. The talk show biz may not be all that glamorous - but the colorful characters I had opportunity to work with made up for that.

My Bay Path University writers community – Michele Barker, Sarah Chadwick, Kathy Garvey, Beth Kenny, Melva Michaelia, Marianne Power, and our beloved muse of a teacher, Suzanne Strempek-Shea. You not only welcomed me when I moved to the great Pioneer Valley, but you inspired me one month at a time, one word at a time.

Adrianne Stone-Gibilisco for her friendship, writer's sensibility, and keen intuition.

The Talkers team: Marcia Daly for her graphics contribution; Mike Kinosian for his supreme command of the language of our business; and Barbara Kurland for her amazing attention to detail.

Matthew B. Harrison and his wife Meghan Harrison for all the heart and help they brought to this project. Thank you for teaching me about "mishpocheh" in this enterprise called family.

Finally, a special thanks to my Duncan siblings – Steve, Phil and Veronica – for being "guests" (sometimes unwittingly) on my original "talk shows" when growing up.